PRAISE

YOU CAN POSTPONE ANYTHING BUT LOVE

and a new era of enlightened parenting

YOU CAN
POSTPONE
ANYTHING
BUT LOVE

RANDALL COLTON ROLFE

WARNER BOOKS

A Warner Communications Company

Warner Books Edition
This Warner Books edition is published by arrangement with the author.

Warner Books, Inc., 666 Fifth Avenue, New York, NY 10103

Ⓦ A Warner Communications Company

Printed in the United States of America
First Warner Books Printing: February 1990
10 9 8 7 6 5 4 3 2 1

Library of Congress Cataloging-in-Publication Data

Rolfe, Randy.
    You can postpone anything but love / Randall Colton Rolfe.
        p. cm.
    Reprint. Originally published: Edgemont, Pa. : Ambassador Press,
1985.
    Includes bibliographical references
    ISBN 0-446-39058-5
    1. Parenting.   2. Child rearing.   3. Child psychology.   4. Love.
I. Title.
[HQ755.8.R65   1990]
649'.1—dc20   89-38674
                                                         CIP

Book design: H. Roberts
Cover design: Karen Katz

To Jason and Tara
Whose love and laughter made this book possible,
And to my husband, to my mother,
And to the memory of my father.

ACKNOWLEDGMENTS

I want to thank my husband Jay Rolfe, who helped inspire and put into practice the ideas presented in this book. I want also to thank my parents Graeme and Sabin Colton, who let me see from the beginning what joy being a parent can bring.

I wish to express my appreciation to my editor Joann Davis, to my publisher Warner Books, and to my agent Ruth Wreschner. I also want to thank all those who helped me to first launch the book under the Ambassador Press imprint.

I am very grateful to the following people who kindly read all or portions of the manuscript at various stages and gave me their thoughts and encouragement: Peter Bergson, Gail Berke, Sam Bruttomesso, Ellen Trescher Haas, Donald Kauffman, Dick and Susan Ostien, Perry Ottenberg, Ian Scott, and Mark Stern.

Finally, I want to note the special inspiration I found in the works of La Leche League International, A. S. Neill, Gregory Bateson, Scott and Helen Nearing, Richard Leakey, Norman Vincent Peale, Frederick Leboyer, and Thomas Powers. Their upbeat attitude towards life and humanity helped me to see the great and still largely untapped potential of parenting in the modern world.

CONTENTS

Foreword		*xi*
Preface		*xiii*
Introduction: High-Need Parents		*xix*
PART I *The Operating Principles*		1
O.P.	1 Spirituality	3
O.P.	2 Love	8
O.P.	3 Validation	12
O.P.	4 Observation	18
O.P.	5 Abstraction	21
O.P.	6 Referencing	27
O.P.	7 Allowance	30
O.P.	8 Trust	34
O.P.	9 Guidance	40
O.P.	10 Expectation	46
O.P.	11 Receptivity	52
O.P.	12 Imitation	58
PART II *The Child's Life Activities*		67
Chapter	1 Sleeping	69
Chapter	2 Eating	76

Chapter 3 Bathing and Cleaning   83
Chapter 4 Dressing   88
Chapter 5 Using the Toilet   91
Chapter 6 Exploring Sex   97
Chapter 7 Helping   104
Chapter 8 Playing   108
Chapter 9 Learning   114
Chapter 10 Socializing   124
Chapter 11 Working   131
Chapter 12 Shopping   136
Chapter 13 Watching Television   140
Chapter 14 Communicating   145
Chapter 15 Healing   154
Chapter 16 Understanding Death   160
Chapter 17 Making Music   164
Chapter 18 Moving   167
Chapter 19 Traveling   170
Chapter 20 Laughing   174
Chapter 21 Living and Loving   177

Suggested Reading   181
Index   187

FOREWORD

This book, "You Can Postpone Anything But Love—Expanding Our Potential as Parents," reflects a crystal clear mind, numerous engaging techniques of child care, and a spiritual dimension that is all too often omitted from the do-it-yourself child-rearing field. My pleasure in reading this book comes from a sense of devotion, sharing, patience, and firmness that the author reflects on every page. I'm always impressed when I meet someone bigger than life who doesn't go halfway to meet the needs of other people but 98% of the way.

Currently in the United States there is a popular interest in spiritual matters, reflecting both collective and individual concerns. This readable book reflects these concerns and will be a welcome addition to the self-help literature that can assist in the lifetime commitment necessary to developing a loving family.

Of course, there are sorrows as well as joys in parenthood. Ms. Rolfe's exploration of ways to bring joy to parenthood does not, of course, imply that a commitment to love can fulfill all the demands of the family. Social realities can fracture any society or family. When these trials occur, experts versed in biological determinism and the stages of child development are needed to sort out the complex effects on personality. But Ms. Rolfe's decision not to focus on these complexities does not negate their importance. Rather, it reflects her concern that many modern parents underrate the importance of being parents and instead try futilely to be mini-experts themselves.

Ms. Rolfe focuses on the salutary applications of that love which is uniquely the business of parents. With the sensitivity and devotion she urges in this book, it may be hoped that parents will be quick to recognize when expert help is needed. Then the unique parental love which this book is about can work hand-in-hand with the work of experts for the good of every child.

> Perry Ottenberg, M.D.
> Senior Attending Psychiatrist
> Institute of Pennsylvania Hospital
> Philadelphia, Pennsylvania

PREFACE

MY husband and I waited eight years before having our children, not an unusual pattern for those who reached maturity in the sixties. We had all the new choices as a result of women's lib and the burgeoning science and service industries. And we had to consider world tensions and increasing complexities of modern family life. Waiting until we felt really ready and eager made sense. Unknowingly, but like many of our contemporaries, we formed definite opinions about our own upbringing, the stories we heard or watched unfold from other families and our own frequent reading. We knew what we did not want, we had inklings about what we did want, but we were pretty fuzzy about how to avoid the first and to encourage the second.

Luckily, our children filled in those gaps, along with more reading and a lot of wonderful sharing with other families. I am grateful that we were open enough, when our first child arrived, to give him the space he needed to teach us what we needed to know to meet his needs as they arose. The most striking thing in the first days was the single-mindedness with which he went after life. Life was really to be loved, sought after, embraced.

Life was very clearly a spiritual experience, as well as a physical and emotional one.

As he grew, acquaintances would say, "What a friendly, cheerful, well-behaved boy—and so bright! You really lucked out this time, but wait until the next one!" We smiled to ourselves that it was not just luck, but we kept our mouths closed because only the second would tell.

Both of us being over-educated with multiple degrees, we were easily overwhelmed with the resources available to dissect, inspect, detect, etc., our child. We knew we would die of confusion or lack of sleep if we attacked parenting with the same kind of research we used for legal issues or biochemical mysteries. Instead we took the leap and decided that our strategy toward parenting would be to relax and enjoy it. But we discovered that we needed a well-thought-out program if we were going to be able to catch ourselves in time to say and do what we really meant to, even when we were feeling tired, hassled, bewildered, self-pitying, or overworked. Our planning paid off. I began to wonder if we had anything we could write down and share with others. But I thought we had better wait for the second child.

Our second child was every bit as helpful in her upbringing as the first. Raised by the same techniques, she elicited the same accolades from acquaintances. But this time they said, "What do you do that makes them so pleasant?"

I am always tempted to say, "Oh, just discipline, discipline, discipline!" to see what they would say. But I always ended up saying something wishy-washy like, "We focus on their self-respect." Now I say, instead, "I hope you will want to read my book!"

Our lives have not been without trial. Our daughter had a life-threatening medical condition which required many weeks in the hospital in her first year. She came through without any complication and inspired us with her own love of life and her infant gusto. Our parenting techniques never failed us.

But acquaintances said, "What a trial—you must have been worried to death! Did you get desperate at times? You must have felt depressed, helpless, scared through all of that." This time we did speak up. "No," we said, "we had our mutual strength, Jason's support, Tara's feisty example, one of the best medical teams in the world, the love of friends and family, and our own faith to carry us on, so that all our energies went into supporting Tara. We simply did not have time for negativity!" It was this experience that allowed us to discover what our special approach to parenting really meant to us and might mean to others. We realized that the charmed life of young professionals was not the only situation in which our parenting program would work.

This book is no substitute for expert advice, or for the many fine books by experts. It is meant as an inspiration to parents to focus specifically on the special role of parents that sets us apart from anyone else in our children's lives and to strive to appreciate the good in ourselves as well as in our children. I hope this book will help return to parents the confidence, hope, trust and joy that I believe we were meant to have for the good of the children.

LOVE

By love I do not mean natural tenderness, which is in people according to their constitution, but I see it as a larger principle of the soul, founded in reason and spiritual understanding, which makes us kind and gentle to all our fellow creatures as creations of God.

—WILLIAM LAW

High-Need Parents

THAT bright fall day, I couldn't wait to get home. I had just finished the last day of my appointment as the attorney and co-author of a federal study on urban air pollution control. It was a compromise job, requiring only forty hours a week. Sixty had been expected of me when I had been a corporate litigation lawyer before my kids were born.

That day I was eagerly looking forward to spending more time with my four-year-old son and my two-year-old daughter while I looked for my next job.

"You can postpone anything but love!" I thought to myself. Hundreds of thoughts rushed through my mind in response to that simple idea. They were the same as the ones I've heard from thousands of women in the teaching and counseling I've done since that important fall day. In trying to combine full-time mothering with a full-time career, I faced the same challenges as a whole generation of women. As a result, my parenting relationship had special needs.

We currently dedicate more of our time to non-family work than any generation of women before us. Government records show that in 1973 half of the women with school-age children were in the labor force. By 1983, the proportion was two-thirds.

What's more, the late eighties were a time when more women of pre-schoolers and infants are working outside the home than ever before. Over 1.7 million mothers with children under one year old were in the labor force in 1985, according to Census Bureau figures. That's nearly half, or 48.4 percent, of all new mothers aged 18 to 44. The figure is over 50 percent for the first-time mothers who are college-educated and over 30 years old.

In contrast, less than one-third, or 31 percent, of new mothers worked outside the home in 1976. In 1980, it was still only 38 percent.

Changes in family patterns have seldom been so dramatic. But there is more.

We are doing all this at older ages. Many of our generation, the baby-boomers, are just now having children. Society, not to mention our parents, has been waiting a long time for the coming of this second baby boom—the grandbaby boom.

In nineteen eighty-seven, a record number of children were born to Americans, 3,000,829. And a greater portion of these than any time this century were born to mothers over 30. The number of children born to women aged 35 to 39 went up 18 percent in 1982 alone, and has continued to climb. Meanwhile, the rate of births to mothers in their twenties has declined.

Why have we waited so long to have kids? And what are our special needs as parents?

Like so many women who grew up in the sixties, I was encouraged to look down on women who were "just housewives." Women's lib told us our mothers were victims, even if we never really got that impression from them. We entered careers, we fought for our rights, we established our value in the marketplace, and we defined ourselves as persons first, women second.

We became persons of ambition for our mothers, persons of principle for our fathers, and collectors of goods, friends, successes, and experiences for ourselves. We wanted to prove ourselves, to go where no woman had gone before, to experience all there is in life. In our desire to deny any biological imperatives, to change tradition, to be our own boss, many of us put off kids.

We had many reasons.

A participant in Earth Day and getting in touch with your Self, I wanted to wait for a natural urge for children, and it didn't come until I was near thirty. Also, I wanted to know where I was going before I took responsibility for guiding someone else.

It's taken longer for our generation than for most to decide that we are adults, ready to have children. Many of us just didn't want to be like our mothers, but we didn't know any other way to be grown up. So we denied the whole process for a while and continued to collect experiences.

I also had grave concerns about the state of the world. Sixties children were deeply aware of the nuclear threat, world shortages, urban congestion, pollution, numerous sex issues, drug abuse and more. As David Elkind points out in *The Hurried Child*, these pressures intrude ever earlier into children's lives.

I also secretly wondered if a committee of experts could do better raising children than I could. Our own mothers went to experts as a last resort. Today expert opinion on every possible problem comes to us before we even know we have a problem. We think to be a parent we need to be mini-experts—from baby-sitter to teacher, confessor, chauffeur, nurse, psychiatrist, coach, friend, judge, pharmacist or tutor.

Some of my friends decided not to have children at all.

Yet seemingly against the odds, most of us still do decide to be parents. Often those who have decided against it change their minds. Why?

Putting off children left me lots of time to get to know my husband, to build my marriage, my career, my confidence. But I soon found a down side to the liberated career-oriented life of the seventies women and the two-income couple. All the external liberation had not liberated me from internal pressures, nor even given me the external satisfaction I expected.

I found the workaday world grueling and often boring. Like Casanova, the conquest was all. Once I landed the job and the respect, sticking with a job that demanded all my waking hours and all my loyalty weighed heavily. I secretly wondered if men really had it as good as we had been led to believe. I felt there had to be more to life.

And all of our efforts still haven't brought us any improvement in prosperity or quality of life over that of our parents. The Associated Press reports that even with the drastic increase in two-income families, median family income in real terms has been going down steadily since 1973. In 1984 dollars, median family income was at $28,167 in 1973 and was down to $26,433 in 1984. It continues to decline.

Now that we are in our thirties and forties, we wonder still how to define ourselves and where we are going. We are leaders of the self-help movement. We spend our paychecks on therapy. We seek answers in metaphysics and other disciplines outside the scientific and rational world that we were so pleased to become a respected part of. Cynics accuse us of collecting healing experiences the same way we collected our earlier experiences.

We've been disparagingly called a nation of adolescents, seeking approval from employers rather than from within, going in all directions rather than sticking with commitments, experimenting endlessly rather than making choices, collecting experiences rather than living as if right now mattered. For some, parenting does begin as just one more experience we decide we must have. Or it is a last-ditch effort to find out who we are and what we are here for.

There is surely some of the biological imperative.

But we have a deeper reason for having our children. When we choose to have children, we are expressing an important new faith in ourselves and in the future.

With so many reasons to wait and then to go forward, we are a generation with uniquely high expectations of parenting. We want so much to do it perfectly, to avoid all the mistakes we think our parents, friends, or media personalities have made.

We are tempted to go at parenting just as we would approach a project at work. We assemble the research, make choices, delegate parts to those we think most capable, and manage the project prudently and rationally. We feel devastated to find that this doesn't feel like enough.

We expect a lot of our children too. We look to them for love, and for a deeper understanding of life itself. We look to them as a cap to an already full life. You might call us "high-need parents." We want a lot from our children, for our children, for ourselves. Like high-need children, we will not let our dreams be denied. And we have been trained in the marketplace to never say die, to work compulsively toward our goals and to experience extreme frustration and guilt when we appear to be failing.

Like so many mothers with whom I've talked, the power of the parenting experience took me by surprise. I was expecting a rich, engaging experience, a glimpse into the future, a new lease on life. Only I found something else, something I never expected or even believed existed. Something outside myself and inside myself at the same time. Something that set my well-ordered priorities on their ear, made my jobs pale to insignificance as sources of self-esteem, made me question my most well-reasoned goals, made me ask why I had waited so long.

I discovered now.

On that fall day I realized that I had the rest of my life to "work," but no more than ten years to give the bulk of my input as a parent, ten years to broadcast my parental love at maximum volume. I resolved that as soon as I could, I would develop work that I could do at home, to be available to my children, to share their young lives with them. With the capabilities we've developed as eighties women, once we set our minds to something, it often comes true sooner than we think. It did for me.

I felt some embarrassment at first that with all my modern freedom I was right where the old patterns would have predicted. I was moving heaven and earth to be home with my children. But there was a difference. I felt it, and others, I noticed, did too—even my old law professors. I had not gone backward. I had gone forward. I had made a free choice based on my personal insight into what was right for me. In fact, I was making many many choices, new every day.

Parenting is the oldest profession. But it is new to each person who enters it. And today we have even fewer real-life models than in prior eras. Nuclear family patterns isolated us as never before from other branches of the family where we might have seen parenting. And we even missed watching our parents with our younger siblings, because we were universally sent to school as soon as we were old enough to consciously remember anything.

If we look to the media for our models, we read about women

who appear to have it all. We feel guilty about not being able to do it all ourselves, about biting off more than we can chew, about leaving some of our new rights unexercised, about being less emotionally independent than we think we ought to be, about feeling a strong pull to family after all.

In our effort not to be traitor to our strident assertions as young career women, we hang on to our old rationalizations for avoiding traditional paths. We tell ourselves that kids don't require so much parental time, that putting family number one is boring and stifling, that the men who were gone all day had the advantage in self-fulfillment. But just because we can be corporate presidents, must we? Just because we don't have to be home with our kids, can't we feel good about being there if we want to?

If we turn to our experts, we hear many who tell us daycare is safe, parents need to get away, family is not totally fulfilling to healthy modern women, kids can take the stresses of modern life as well or better than we can.

Can we believe this? And do we really want to?

I once shared the podium on a call-in show with a young obstetrician. A mother called in to say that she felt torn. She didn't feel right about leaving her six-month-old son while she took a getaway week with her husband, but she knew her parents would take good care of him, and her husband wanted it.

The obstetrician said she needed the rest, it was good for her marriage and she shouldn't worry. But there were tears in the mother's voice that told me that she needed someone to give her permission to respect her feelings, to follow her instincts. She was looking for permission to assert her motherly right to stay home.

The young obstetrician was well-educated and knowledgeable. But she had never been a mother, never bonded with a child, never even been a wife. Can we expect experts to tell us what is best for us if they have never had a baby?

What's more unsettling, can we expect experts who do have children to reach unbiased conclusions in their studies about parents' and children's needs when they work full time themselves outside the home and naturally desire to believe that their life choices aren't harming their child or making them miss anything?

Further, much of the body of expert opinion about parenting has been the product of full-time professional men, who have never been mothers, nor have they been expected to bond with or spend time with their young children until recently. Can we expect them to explore the special value of a relationship in which parent and child are regularly available to each other when they personally have never felt it, may not be able to recognize it and often even doubt that it exists?

The brain waves of a mother and her nursing infant are closer than any two human beings other than identical twins. Have our experts allowed the full ramifications of this discovery to alter their conclusions about how parents and children relate best to each other?

Shopping for experts can be as discouraging as trying to find solutions by ourselves. And there are few other places to turn.

In his new book *Family and Nation*, Senator Daniel P. Moynihan describes how the needs of family have been unmet by modern society. In our drive to be active participants in society at large, we have unknowingly belittled, avoided and kept ourselves unaware of the attractions, emotional comforts, needs and social importance of family.

The nineties will be a time when the family is rediscovered. Our generation is building a new family where each member appreciates why he or she is there and why the others are there too. It's a family where continuous dialogue, using the language of relationship, self-esteem, interdependence, cooperation and personhood reaffirms the essential value of each member. Just in the few years since my bright fall day of decision, progress has been phenomenal.

As in so many other areas of our lives, we have few guides. But we do have one another. The courageous choices of others inspire us and give us the courage to choose for ourselves in parenting as in other areas. We also can learn from our children.

With our extensive education, careers and life experience, it is hard for us to accept that our children can teach us much. We think we know it all. But we are more able than ever to benefit from the mutual learning process of the parenting relationship. We bring so much to it.

I discovered in my children the importance of now. A child won't wait. We may label it impatience, immaturity, excessive neediness, unsettling egocentricity. But it is none of these. The child's unwillingness to wait is a gift to us that we can keep on giving for the rest of our lives.

Children keep growing whether you are there or not. They take their first step whether it is you or someone else holding their hand. Life unfolds for them without a schedule-minder, three-year goals or report cards. If we aren't there they learn as much as if we are there, only different things.

Kids *will* wait for a new house, a new bed, a vacation, an A-plus, a met deadline, new clothes, new toys, better food, new friends, better books, more money. What they won't wait for is love. They won't wait for attention, sharing time together, affirmation of personal worth, validation of well-meaning effort, celebration of life, affectionate touching, emotional security, compassion, gentle words, encouragement in learning, food, shelter or health. These come only with parental love, and our children will let us know if we postpone it.

I made a decision on that fall day not to postpone love. I had heard so many times from parents that children grow up too fast. Too fast for what? Once I had my own children I understood. It was too fast to love enough. On that day I was determined not to have to live with that feeling. I had to love them now. I resolved to enjoy my children so much every day that I would be comfortable with the rate of their growth. I was determined to have no regrets attributable to careless postponing of parental love.

We choose not to postpone love when we ignore advice and stay with our children at night as long as they want, even when it takes forty minutes. We choose not to postpone love when we leave hungry guests to nurse a baby.

We choose not to postpone love when we take our infant to the board meeting of an international cultural exchange group. We choose not to postpone love when we comfort, empathize and remind, rather than scold, ignore and punish. We choose not to postpone love when we take our child's side on the question of unnecessary homework.

We choose not to postpone love when we conclude that in seeking happy children we are not giving up the promise of successful children. We choose not to postpone love when we interpret insistence on more toys as a plea for more time, resistance at mealtime as a cry for more attention, rebellion at bedtime as a prayer for more family calm.

We choose not to postpone love when we realize that our old goal was not to get away from family but to have the freedom to stay or go by our own best choice. We choose not to postpone love when we resist the urge to run for a camera to memorialize something for the future and instead enjoy it fully in the moment.

This book is about how to actively live as if love were a real force in your daily family life. Because it is. Love is not a reward that is postponed while we please our parents, obey our teachers, satisfy our boss, pacify our spouse, educate our children or entertain ourselves. It is a process in which we actively participate, consciously or not, every day. To use its power takes time, commitment and lots of practice. It doesn't lend itself to being an after-hours alternative.

Certainly the complexities of modern life burden parents mercilessly. But our lives do offer us all the opportunities we need, except for those gripped by the most severe social distortions at the extremes of society.

To find out how to apply the power of our parental love, we need to begin by taking a look at what we really want from our parenting. Then we can order our lives to help bring it about.

We parents seem to share three basic goals. First, we want to enjoy our parenting—to minimize the hard or sad times and maximize the happy ones, ending up proud of the great effort we put out.

Second, we want to raise children who will know how to make life happy and worthwhile for themselves.

And third, we want to prepare them to cope with their world and to leave it in as good or better shape than when they came.

These goals seem at times to conflict or interfere with one another. When we want to have a good time with our children, we feel guilty that they are not learning anything useful. When they are being educated, we worry that the style of instruction is detracting from their self-esteem. When we are building their value base, we worry that they are becoming too serious.

In this book you will see how when we keep our eye on the basics of our relationship, these goals reinforce one another and are essential one to the other. Like other goals, they serve more for direction than as a prize in the end. They are ongoing processes that we must take the time to facilitate throughout our lives.

This book is the result of my personal quest for a fulfilling life as a parent. In it I seek to pass on to you what I have learned—thoughts, attitudes, words and actions that I have found useful. In my workshops with other mothers I have seen the pandemic anxiety in modern parenting. Most often this anxiety is not because we are maladjusted parents. Nor is it because our children are bad or misguided.

It is because we know so little about parenting. We make choices off-the-cuff, we wing it, we talk off the top of our heads, we shoot from the hip. One minute we grab something from old mental tapes of our parents. Another minute we borrow something from a Phil Donahue show. The next minute we try to do the opposite of what we saw a girlfriend do with her child last week.

This book aims to give you the basic support you need to make the right choices for you. You'll be asked to take a hard look not at your child, nor at your own underlying psychological makeup, but rather at the relationship between you and your child. This is a book about parenting style—what do you say and do that sets the tone for your parenting relationship.

You will learn basic operating principles for anticipating the results of your choices. And the second half of the book is practical examples of how different styles will affect your family relationships in a number of everyday family acitivities.

It is meant to be a practical book that can be used again and again. It is also a reflection of my profound conviction that in order to speak and act consistently with your personal values and goals, you must ground your approach in some basic, often ignored truths about relationships, children, parents and people.

I came at these through the back door, trying to make some sense out of a hodgepodge of parenting strategies, advice and philosophies. I was not trained in child development or psychology, but applied myself to synthesize much material that was already available and to make it work for me.

The ideas in this book are a very personal synthesis, combining the essence of modern programs for improving communication between people with the practical techniques of ancient spiritual systems for leading a more meaningful life. They are also consistent with modern scientific knowledge about how and why learning occurs and what makes us special as human beings.

By getting to know ourselves as parents and by watching ourselves as closely as we watch our children, we can expand our potential as parents beyond the multiple roles as mini-experts that we too often try to assume. The most rewarding life for both child and parent will emerge when we put first things first and focus our energies on just being parents.

Unlike a job where it is possible to follow in another's footsteps, parenting touches our deepest sensibilities and brings out our personal uniqueness. If we do not recognize this and instead try to follow in others' footsteps, we find frustration, confusion and disappointment.

If we are tempted to put off getting our own heads together until we are through the hard years with our children, those hard years may drag on far longer than need be. If we are wrapped up in our own expectations, little guilts, self-admonitions and unexamined emotions, or in controlling, suspecting and second-guessing our children—when we are really suspecting ourselves—we will find it almost impossible to notice and enjoy the spontaneous revelations in the daily life of the average child. We will sadly shortchange ourselves as well as our children.

Instead, we need to welcome parenting as a valuable nudge to come to terms with ourselves and what makes us unique, so that we can then love our children as ourselves. It is a hard truth that if you aren't enjoying your parenting, your child isn't enjoying being a child. Now is the time to make sure that you postpone anything but love.

If this appears too demanding of the parent, consider how

much time and effort parents expend on children already. We drive them here and there, buy their favorite cereals, argue with them, worry about how to discipline them, defend their actions against volunteer critics, wonder whether to call for help, fret about their future, interview sitters and schools, and rationalize away attacks of guilt. Most parents are devoted to their children and already spend an incredible amount of time and energy on them, if not with them.

With the help of this book, you can now spend that same time and energy in a more positive, enjoyable, loving way.

Parenting involves *all* of ourselves. There are parts our children won't let us delegate no matter how hard we try. Whether they show it right away or not, our children are responsive to our every word and deed.

It is easy to feel scared by the awesome power we have as parents. But children are forgiving. Any errors, whether we know what they are or not, whether they were ours or someone else's, whether they can be corrected easily or only with years of therapy, deserve forgiveness and can almost always be healed.

Many well-meaning advisors recommend denying our power in order to avoid guilt feelings if children don't turn out the way we want. But guilt is a feeling like any other. It is suppressed at our peril. If we deny that we can help cause problems, then we end up denying that we have the power to help prevent them. In exchange for temporary guilt avoidance, we face a future of searching for solutions to problems we might have prevented. It is a sad thought how much pain is imposed on children by parents who are denying their power in order to minimize guilt.

You cannot really avoid guilt that way anyway. It only migrates. If Joan is convinced that little Melinda's sassiness has nothing to do with eight hours of day-care and a frazzled mother at dinner, Joan still is not guilt-free. She still feels guilty—that she can't spend more time with the psychologist, that she can't change the way Melinda's brother treats her, or that she is somehow a failure as a mom.

The only way to be free of guilt over a relationship is to know in your heart you have done your best in that relationship. And this you achieve only if you give your love now.

I hope you will find with the help of this book the words and actions that will be most useful to you in building the loving parental relationship that is most satisfying to you. You will find techniques of thinking that will allow you to say and do creative, appropriate and loving things, even when your mind is clouded with worry, impatience, hurt, anger, guilt, distrust or misunderstanding. And you will learn how to tell where you end and your child begins in any situation, so that you know when to speak or act and when to be still.

The twelve pragmatic concepts I call operating principles in Part I give a foundation where you can build new perceptions and interpretations, new habits and patterns, new options and opportunities, and new relationships and parenting styles.

These principles are not rules that we must obey for a certain result. They are more like the laws of Nature. We cannot disobey them. They operate independently. Yet we can use them consciously to improve our family relationships if we take them into account as we make our daily choices.

The family activities in Part II are meant to be suggestive of the wide range of choices available to us in any family situation. Choices seldom are dependent on the sex and age of the child. If we speak and act without special allowances for age and sex but only with normal sensitivity to the other's level of comprehension and interest, we show our respect for the uniqueness of each child. We treat the child like another person, not a special breed of person.

This allows the child's own personality—physical, intellectual, emotional, biochemical, spiritual, perceptual, sensual, sexual and interpersonal—to emerge genuinely and change positively without the extra burden of our expectations, old patterns and stereotypes.

Likewise, the sex and age of the parent don't affect the usefulness of the suggestions in this book. Parents of both sexes, single parents, stepparents and even grandparents use them with personal success. The misconceived picture of the father as distant protector and the mother as the prime nurturer arose as a rationale in support of the regrettable absenteeism of the father in the industrial era. The mass entry of mothers into the labor force, the more flexible work schedules of fathers in the service and computer industries and the increase of single-parent families has helped fathers rediscover their nurturing side. A recent study concluded that it is neither sex nor cultural stereotype that determines the nurturing quality of a parent. It is rather the situation and opportunity. The study found single fathers of the eighties just as nurturing as mothers of the fifties.

Of course there are always differences in parenting styles and shared activities within each family. We do not seek unisex parenting. Distinctions based on the family members as people, not as roles, form the foundation for genuine, trustful and lasting relationships. It is just as important to the parenting relationship for the personality of the father and mother to emerge genuinely as it is for the child's to do so.

Most of the examples in this book that involve babies will speak of the mother as parent because she usually will share more activities with a child in the first year or two of life, even if the father is at home, and especially if the mother and baby breastfeed. But even in the first years the father is more important than is commonly supposed. If you work with the suggestions in this book, you will come to appreciate how much influence a father has, even if only changing a diaper, adjusting a seatbelt or cuddling the baby to sleep.

This book will ask you to focus on techniques of responding to your children's wants and needs as they express them. This is the central activity of parents and it is more than enough to keep us busy. Also, it is all we can expect to have any confidence about. As you respond to expressed needs and wants as best you know how, you will see communication improve because you are rewarding it, making your child feel strong and effective, and the child will begin to help you become the parent you want to be.

When we do the exercises that try to read the minds of children, imagining all their thoughts and feelings, it is only to demonstrate these three things: First, that their inner life is just as important, sensitive, and sophisticated as any adult's. Second, that each child is so complex and unique that it is impossible for us to imagine or guess at any given time what they are thinking.

And third, that it is even more hopeless to think we can control their inner lives.

Our best bet is to treat our children as we would most like to be treated ourselves if we were new people, inexperienced, eager for life and preprogrammed for love. Putting ourselves in their place this way may not be as difficult as we think. I have found it a wonderful relief because then and only then do we get a sense of how to meet their greatest needs best. Even with all our experience, and I believe largely because of it, we are high-need parents. Our inner life is as impatient for love as our child's.

If we rid ourselves of the burden of second-guessing and controlling our children's inner lives, we will release ourselves from many illusory duties and will use our energy for building a relationship and parenting style that can fulfill our parenting goals every day and guide our children toward their highest potential, which may well be beyond our imagining.

Great parents run the gamut from home-bodies to jet-setting power-brokers and everything between. This book is meant to counteract the vague anxiety that high-need parents often feel. Our generation is uniquely prone to couple a generalized anxiety over not giving enough to our child with a subtle suppression of the urge to just love him. This book will help you let go of anxiety and indulge the love urge.

This book is a counterbalance to all the anti-parent hoopla—that mixing kids and career successfully is only a matter of scheduling and management, that a professionally active mother will surely make a better mother, that day-care is as good as home, that absentee fathers have been the lucky ones and that quality time can substitute for quantity.

Here are a few of the parent-affirming ideas I have gleaned from my own experience, confirmed by the experience of thousands of other parents who have used the suggestions in this book:

> Your intuition and parental instincts are good and
>   reliable.
> You will lose nothing by changing your mind about
>   priorities.
> You know your child best.

You have no obligation to live with guilt.
Your child needs you, just because you are you.
You need no one's permission to do what feels right for
    your child and yourself.
You can give your children more time than you ever
    dreamed of without hurting them or yourself.

What about economics, pressure for education, demands of jobs and chosen ways of life?

Once these parent-affirming ideas become comfortable for you, you may find that you will want to change your lifestyle, environment, income or whatever, as need be, to accommodate new priorities. You can press into service all your workplace experience, successes and maturity toward this end. None of these is ever lost in becoming a parent today, whether you keep a job or not.

Options you never dreamed of before may materialize. Extra time with your child may be attainable. And more of your time will be of higher quality than you may have thought possible. I like to remember the Roman rule: The one who says it cannot be done should never interrupt the one who is doing it.

With a little faith and a lot of mutual reinforcement, my husband, too, has made the changes necessary to spend time with his children while they are young. The impossible just takes a little longer.

I believe our families have the power and the opportunity to change both internal patterns and society's responses more creatively and supportively than ever before. I hope this book will help strengthen our common resolve to do so. Use this book again and again to help bolster your confidence that all of us are capable of making important contributions to the lives of our children no matter how little time, training or money we have.

I suggest you read this book through and then try, a little at a time, to put the suggestions to work. Small and surprising changes will happen almost immediately, with the full potential of the approach beginning to show itself after about three months. After that, the sky is the limit.

As high-need parents, we seek both an enlightened and

enlightening parenting relationship. Like a high-need child whose first responsibility is to insist that his needs are met, our first responsibility is to insist that our needs are met. We do not need to wait for permission to follow our best intuitions. We can feel good now about doing what feels right for our family. And we can postpone anything but love.

I hope together we can reassert the best of our generation's ideals while rejecting the worst of our self-serving rationalizations. As we build our new families into the nineties, I hope we will work toward generating the kind of personal and societal changes that will make parenting easier in the twenty-first century.

Being a parent myself and knowing how low a priority reading can be at times, I have tried to write the book to be read piecemeal if need be. Pick it up when a little child is dozing off in your arms, when your son is playing with the cat or when your daughter is blowing soap bubbles. If they need you, please put it down for another time.

But don't be reluctant to ask an older child for the time to do some reading just for you, and for your relationship. This book is not to change your child, to make her better. She will do that on her own with your help as you integrate the ideas in this book into your life. The book is to change you, to make you happier.

I am eager to learn what this book means to you and what applications you find. Please let me know! And good luck!

You Can
Postpone
Anything
But Love

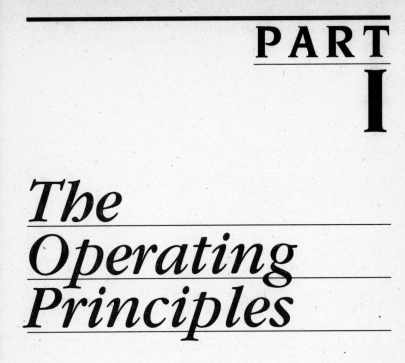

PART
I

The
Operating
Principles

All the love we come to know in life springs
from the love we knew as children.
—*Thomas J. Langley*

Spirituality

The child is essentially a spiritual being

PARENTS are the only ones in the world who have brand-new people put completely under their care. We parents must be something special. What is expected of us? Is there any way to find out? Is trying to remember what our parents did with our little brother, or watching what the neighbor does, or reading what another parent finds helpful our only way to find who we are as parents?

With so many different bits of advice, cultural traditions, academic studies, and more, it would seem wise to try to get down to real basics. What is this baby anyhow? If we can figure out what she is, perhaps we will be able to determine exactly what we are supposed to do with her.

At the moment of birth, most parents find that their newborn child is surprisingly whole, strong-willed, confident, and expectant. We notice quickly that she accepts no excuses which are based on non-essential considerations, like the phone ringing, the undone housework, or the unread mail. We find that she responds totally and unabashedly to the essentials of life, like warmth, nourishment, touching, sleeping, natural rhythmic motion (like our breathing), smiles, laughter, and her own natural functions and reflexes.

The newborn seems to be already a whole person, somehow split off from the overall unity of life whose force must have brought us all into being. Whether we designate this force as God or in some other way is not so important for our purposes here as is our recognition that the child is a unique manifestation of life, having at her core the spirituality which distinguishes life from a stone. Some basic qualities of life which we can see in our newborn are: energy, vibrance, radiance, goodwill, growth, change, balance, and a guileless responsiveness to the essence of things.

It is this spiritual element which many families seek when they take special care to have a childbirth experience with no unnecessary interventions and among familiar people and surroundings. But many families too have found this element without seeking it. They wanted only a natural birth and did not anticipate its spiritual side. Yet parents, friends, and obstetricians alike attest to the essentially spiritual nature of the birth, akin to a sacrament. This spirituality continues after birth into infancy and childhood, and hopefully it will continue throughout our child's life.

If our newborn is a unique spiritual being put into our care, we parents are uniquely placed in position to exert the first and strongest influence on the growth of that being—his physical, emotional, mental and spiritual growth. What tools should we use to carry out this responsibility? And can we expect to enjoy it?

New attitudes toward adult growth shed light on the life of our child. No longer do we assume that a period of learning in childhood is routinely followed by a static life as householder and professional which ends in grandparenthood and retirement. Our new awareness of life's passages and mid-life crises have eliminated the idea that any person is static. Our children are surely moving a lot faster than the rest of us, but still they move along the same path, by the same rules.

We need to abandon the idea that children are a special kind of human and instead give them the benefit of both modern techniques of interpersonal communication and ancient techniques for spiritual potentiation which religious leaders have recognized throughout the ages. Scriptures in all religious traditions draw parallels between the attitude of the child and the attitude that a mature adult best adopts to grasp the wonder of life. We can teach our children not through absolute maxims and a finite list of rules, but rather through the everyday expression of our unique caring as parents, using these well-proven techniques in our daily interactions with them.

If we recognize the innate spiritual nature of our children, we must accept that they are basically good. We need not assume the impossible task of forcing them to be good. We can expect them to meet us halfway. Our job is not to create them anew, but to protect them and guide them so that they can build on their basic goodness.

The basic goodness of children is not an idealistic notion to put haloes on the little angels of doting parents. Rather, it agrees with many enlightened observations of human culture and life itself. The individual in any species of life generally behaves in a way most likely to preserve itself and its species. Both instincts from the genes and learning from experience govern these behaviors. Instinct predisposes creatures to increase behaviors which give them pleasant feelings and to decrease behaviors which give them painful feelings. Learning comes about according to the feedback of pain or pleasure which the individual receives from different behaviors. If a species will survive, those behaviors which are most helpful to survival must give pleasant feelings and must be easily learned.

Learning is the supreme behavior of human beings which has helped us survive despite the complete dependence of our first several years. That early dependence is actually the means by which the child is exposed to continuous learning from the people around him. Social interaction is the principal means of human behavioral learning. If social interaction and learning are central to the success of the human species, then these behaviors of human beings must give pleasant feelings.

We can expect, then, that our children will be naturally inclined to enjoy learning and social interaction with us. We do not need to force them into it. We must help them develop their inborn desire to cooperate, to love, to be liked, to give others the room to enjoy the same things they enjoy, and to share what they have. We must help them preserve and nurture these innate behavioral tendencies, in a world which at times seems to discourage them. But we do not have to start from scratch.

This line of reasoning seems to agree with the intuition of many parents. Just like the lovemaking and childbirth which preceded it, childrearing is not meant to be a painful, turbulent, mixed blessing. It is supposed to be a spiritually enlightening, physically invigorating, generally happy, and pleasurable experience for parents as well as children. If we dedicate ourselves to finding the good in our children and to bringing it out with well-tested techniques, we well be hard at work at our own enlightenment also. We will find our jobs as parents more rewarding and more joyful than we ever could have imagined.

The basic goodness of children is not some absolute goodness waiting to be corrupted by parents or their world. Rather it is a relative goodness which, when reflected in our working assumptions, helps us think more clearly and respond more positively to our children.

It is awareness of this relative goodness that keeps us parents from drowning in the counterproductive arrogance of imagining ourselves spiritually better than or superior to our children. If we were to assume children were born bad, we could (and often do anyhow) slip into thinking that our superior experience has made us better spiritually than they. It is then far too easy to jump to the assumption that we have a license to second-guess, mold, and control our child's every thought and action. This assumption stifles both us and our children. The idea of God the Almighty Father is a wonderful concept to help give us a more real grasp of the totality of God. But it cannot be rightly turned around to justify I the father, with all my imperfections as a parent, acting like Almighty God by exercising absolute power over my child. Our parenting efforts can at best only build on the innate goodness that already exists in our children.

By putting us on an equal footing spiritually with our children, the recognition of the inherent goodness of children is of value. It is not useful if it makes us swing the other way, making us feel inferior to our children spiritually, so that we feel responsible for their imperfections. None of us can claim total control or responsibility for the life or development of another. Each of us is imperfect, but each of us is a unique attempt at perfection in light of the one perfection that we call God. Parents do not deserve blame if their children are less than perfect. But at the same time, no parent could rightly claim to have made his child better than he was at birth.

If we assume that our child is basically good, we relieve ourselves of the obligation to be always judge of our child. As imperfect as we are, we are in no position to judge or condemn. Whatever our child is, we must respond to the very best we can find in him. When two people are put in the unique relationship of parent and child, one experienced at life and one inexperienced, the experienced one must accept the uniqueness and essential spiritual qualities of the new one and nurture him through his fastest growing and learning years until he is ready to take his life and aspirations into his own hands.

The principle of spirituality means that while our child is born with a "clean slate" as far as worldly experience, she already has an internal program which guides her perception of life, so that what goes onto the slate will not be what we want to go on it so much as what our child perceives must go on it. It will be our job as parents to see that our child's perception remains as clear as possible and that what she sees reinforces and validates her spiritual identity. The other operating principles show how this can come about.

Love

The child experiences
the world through love

AS a spiritual being, the child recognizes from the start that the essence of life is experienced through love. Mother's love is the first human relationship the child experiences, through the immediate smell, feel, taste, sound, sight, and rhythmic vibrations of the mother. All the child experiences from then on will be comprehended first as a message about love. If we consider the child's God-given program as a grid through which experiences are passed in order to find out what the child should learn from them, the first level of the grid contains a standard of love. In fact, at birth, about the only standard on the grid is love. If birth is not too painful and mother is there when birth is over, love will have begun.

Even the apparent self-centeredness of a baby is a sign of total love, if we consider the spiritual nature of the child and the limit of the child's experience so far. The child has only known unity before. She has never before been a conscious individual, separate from that unity. And her only experience of life so far is her own needs and feelings. We need not be surprised, then, that the baby focuses on herself. In fact, it is extremely important to the child's physical survival that she love herself above all. But since the baby is still unaware of her separateness from others, all the world is included in this self-love.

I like to imagine that when a child is born, he first thinks "Love," learned directly from God. This love is not a noun—a thing, but is rather a verb—a process, a becoming, a creation. Then the child adds, "All loves," when he senses the world around him. Then, "We love," when he feels his mother. Then, "I love," when he recognizes his own identity. Then, "They love." Then, "I love me." Then, "I love my mommy." Then, "I love my daddy." And so forth. The sequence need not stop until we or someone or something else causes it to.

Any experience can give an invalidating message, whether it be a death which goes uninterpreted, a warning given too soon to beware of strangers, or some other denial of love. But one or several denials will not negate this innate positive world-view. Like any changing attitude, only cumulative contrary experiences can eventually force a child to give up her positive, hopeful approach to life. As long as the positive experiences predominate over the negative ones, the child will hang on to her positive world-view.

The early years are the most important for confirming the child's positive world-view. The more secure the child is in his perception, the more likely he will be to reach out to life, to feel control over his destiny, and to bring joy to himself and others. Every experience of the child carries with it some message about love. The earlier the experience, the greater the impact.

It is for this reason that the process of toilet training has been a key in psychoanalysis. When we force a child to adopt a particular behavior before the child is ready, we will have a negative impact on the child's world-view. It was universal in Freud's time, and is still fairly common in our own, for parents to assume that toilet training must be pushed, the earlier the better. The child will learn to behave in the desired manner in most cases. But she will also learn something at the level of love. All the scolding, frustration, and coaxing the child will see in the parent and experience in herself may demonstrate that love can be and should be compromised at times. This message has all the more impact because it comes so early in a child's life, may be repeated daily, and relates to basic body functions, which otherwise seem to the child to be merely essential, with no particular value-overlays of any kind.

Freud found that many adult problems, including low self-esteem, inability to take the risks of loving, insecurity, and embarrassment or confusion over vital bodily functions could often be traced to these early wounds to the child's world-view.

In contrast, if the child is allowed to learn behaviors when he seeks to learn them, no negative lessons about love will be learned. Rather, the message will be that we trust the child's sense of timing and his ability to interpret his needs, and we are willing to wait for our cue.

The principle of love means that parents should try to be conscious of what impact each experience may have on the child's world-view and do their best to make it a positive one.

For example, when a child asks a question that we expect to find very difficult to answer, we can first answer it at the world level of love, and often the rest will fall into place with little effort. If Melissa asks, "Why do mommies and daddies kiss like that?" we tend to think, "Oh no, is it time to explain sex already? How much can she comprehend? How can I explain the difference between parental and sexy kisses? Will she lose interest in the middle and be left with the wrong impression?"

But if we view the question as a love question first, we can start very simply: "Mommies and daddies love each other in a special way, because they can have babies like you when they make love to each other. That kind of very close kiss makes them feel good about being married."

If the child is ready for more and is accustomed to having his questions answered, he will ask for more. But if he was just wondering if he should kiss like that, or what it was that daddy was communicating to mommy, that may be enough for now. The child will refine the question to a more precise level if he desires more information. If that is enough for now, we can wait patiently until the child raises the subject again.

Today we tend sometimes to think of love as a passive emotion. We love someone because that person is lovable. Our mass media emphasize romance so much that we tend to think of falling in and out of romantic love as the pattern for love in general. The love a child feels is a very active love. It has less to do with the particular love object than with the attitudes of the loving person. Love as used in this book means seeking and finding the good in others and taking pleasure in it. It includes trust, forgiveness, patience, joy, hope, and many other positive emotions which we focus toward ourselves and others. The child loves before all else, as we shall see further in the examples in Part II.

O. P. 3

Validation

The child seeks validation
of his or her world-view

SINCE the child experiences the world primarily at the
spiritual level and tends toward a loving view of the world,
he will feel best about himself when experiences and
activities validate that world-view. A validating experience
confirms the essential value of the child by demonstrating that
his world-view is valid. Validation of love is the highest reward
in any activity or experience. If we assume that children will seek
experiences which make them feel good, we can see that they
will seek validating experiences. The child experiences validation
through self-love, self-esteem, parental love, familial love, praise,
applause, and the very activity of loving. The kinds of activities
and experiences which a child seeks later in life may well depend
on the validation he received early in life. If the majority of early
experiences validate the child and his loving world-view, that
child will reach maturity with a strong self-validation system
which can help him through the challenges of adult life.

The child knows that "I think: therefore I am" without having ever read the words of the famous philosopher Descartes.
The child senses intuitively that validation of her world-view will
make her feel alive, good, and whole. Since the child senses

herself as a spiritual being, her sense of "self" depends upon having that perception validated. Validation of love gives the important message: "I'm OK!"

The more of this validation a child receives and the earlier, the less he will need it later from others in order to maintain his loving identity, self-confidence, and effectiveness in accomplishing his chosen tasks. Conversely, the less of this validation the child receives and the earlier it is denied, the more he will seek it later from others, and the more insecure and ineffective he will be.

There is a negative side to validation. We might ignore it here, except that it helps explain some otherwise bizarre behavior of children. We often see or hear of children who will not accept positive gestures toward them. They are suspicious and tend to look for the hitch in everything. These are children whose invalidating experiences have predominated over validating ones. They expect that kind words are really a trap to hurt them further when they have opened up a little bit. Those children have a negative world-view and will tend to seek validation of that world-view. They will even misinterpret positive experiences in order to validate that negative world-view.

Discouraging as this may sound, the principle of validation reveals the hopeful side. At least the child still seeks validation, even if it is of a negative world-view. Unlike a child who has developed a strong self-validating system for a positive world-view, a child with a negative world-view will continually seek further validation from the outside.

We might look at this kind of continual seeking as the result of a certain lack of faith. The child with a positive world-view has the faith to carry her through some confusing or discouraging times. But the child with a negative world-view lacks that kind of inner faith, probably because the child's spiritual core senses that the view is unreal. Therefore she needs constant revalidation from the outside to maintain the illusion. Whatever the reason, that child is constantly seeking to prove to herself that her negative view is correct. This means that the negative world-view always has the potential to be turned to a positive one. If the child were content to stay in a no-man's land and think no more about love, or if the spiritual core gave up on ever retrieving a positive world-view, an invalidated child would be permanently lost. But sustained exposure to validating experiences and activities will eventually turn a child around. When the negative world-view no longer receives validation, the child will eventually rethink her world-view and develop a new one which comports with the child's new experience. Patience and acceptance are the key qualities which the helper in this situation needs to cultivate.

On the brighter side, for most of our children, we will not expect them to develop a negative world-view. But we do want to help them develop their own validating system, so that they will not require constantly positive validation from the outside to keep up their spirits when they are on their own. As most of us realize, without the internalized validation system adult life's experiences do not offer constant validation.

It is a common fallacy to conclude from this last thought that family life should mirror adult life and that children should not be validated from the outside any more often than they will be as adults. This is the "They better get used to it now" argument. On the contrary, the self-validation system is more likely to develop more satisfactorily the more consistently the child has been validated in early life.

If this is so, we might wonder whether this means that we cannot say "no" to the child, for fear that it will be a negative experience. In fact, any experience within the life of the family can be validating, no matter how negative it may appear. The other operating principles explain how this is so.

Here, though, we can take a look at how we parents can eliminate some of the confusion by accepting the idea that whether we are saying "no" or "yes" to a particular desire of the child does *not* determine whether the interaction is validating to the child. We sometimes feel confused as to whether we are spoiling a child or simply trying to love and validate the child as often as possible. We spoil a child when we avoid saying "no" because we do not want to displease him and when we exercise license instead of guidance in supervising his activities. Trying to show our love by license and "giving in to the child's every whim" does not validate the child. It may communicate to the child that we want to love the child, but it does not do well in communicating genuine love. Because the child grasps essentials, rather than exactly what we want him to grasp, he may well grasp these invalidating messages in oversolicitous behavior: that we parents want to appear to love the child so badly that we may act contrary to our real love of the child by letting him do things that we know may be harmful to him (like eating ice cream every day); that self-esteem is not an adult characteristic because we parents do not love ourselves enough to draw a line when the child's activities disturb our peace or severely inconvenience us (such as when the noise level is extreme with no signs of stopping or the food is repeatedly spilled); that the child is untrustworthy or incompetent because we do not trust him to appreciate our love except in the form of "bribes"; or that we think license is love.

None of these messages validates any of the spiritual strengths of the child. Rather, they suggest that love is a game of appearances, impressions, and illusions. If this were the nature of most of the child's experiences, she would expect that there was no real love but only its outward appearance. This is the kind of love the child can never internalize, but must perpetually seek from those around her.

Contrary to license, validation calls for saying "no" whenever the child's activities present a risk of permanent harm to the child or unreasonably interfere with the activities and validation of others. Children can grasp that appropriate limits are a sign of love and not an invalidation. It is our job as parents, then, to set appropriate limits and to see that the child perceives the limits we set as appropriate. Awareness of the operating principles will help us to do this.

Even if we have a good understanding of how we parents can validate the child, it is important to be able to recognize when our children are seeking validation. It is very difficult to continue to give validating messages if we misinterpret what the child is doing when he seeks our validation. One of the strongest validations of a parent is eye contact. If we are looking at the child with love and the child knows it and knows that we know it, we have a mutually validating situation. In contrast, if we have been absorbed in other activities, or have been speaking to the child while our attention is partly diverted to something or someone else, we may suddenly find that the child is "putting on a show." Most often this is a call for immediate validation. It is not wrong to give it then and there. Whether the show is laudable or mischievous actually makes little difference in this situation, though when a child needs validation, mischievous things are far easier to think up than laudable ones. Under these circumstances, the principle of validation suggests that rather than punishing the child or ignoring him, we should focus all our attention on the child at the next possible opportunity.

This may take some quick thinking. We do not want to respond positively to the show itself, especially the mischievous one, since this is likely to reinforce the show as an appropriate means of getting our attention. We can try to think of some other reason to focus on the child and minimize the attention-getting behavior itself. For example, we could begin to include the child in our conversation or ask if she would like to help with whatever we are doing. Then we can give the eye contact and attention the child seeks.

But if we cannot think of something fast, the validation should take precedence over the fear of reinforcing the negative behavior. If we accept the event as a reminder to validate the child a bit more often, we should expect that the need to put on a show to get our attention will be less in the future. But the need for validation is a permanent one which we should meet as best we can. Besides, nothing else will bring the mischievous or intrusive behavior to as quick an end.

Praise of a child's good deeds can be validating, but it is important that even if the child is doing nothing good, we still offer him validation. The approval which we parents can give without any performance is often called nonjudgmental love or unconditional love. It does not mean that we cannot take a position on the child's behavior. Rather, it means that we should never attack the child. Our love for the spiritual person in our child should be unconditional and overt.

Traditionally we have assumed that the mother expresses unconditional love while the father dispenses love only for good deeds. There can be no philosophical support for this different approach by the father. It makes no sense at the spiritual level. When self-doubt makes people achieve, their strength must always come from outside rather than inside. Fear of disapproval is not a sign of a mature adult, whose strength comes from within.

Validation as used here means acceptance, approval, and affirmation, as these concepts are used by self-help groups, assertiveness trainers, and psychoanalysts. Validation differs from reinforcement in that reinforcement usually refers to encouragement of precise activities rather than to affirmation of the basic value of a person, but both concepts refer to the idea that people respond best when others recognize and affirm their essential worth. We can do this by listening to them, by trusting in their better nature, and by treating them as equals on the spiritual level. If love is seeking and finding the good in others and taking pleasure in it, validation is what happens to the other who is loved.

Observation

The child observes and
interprets everything

O FTEN a compliment to a child is, "She doesn't miss a thing!" We enjoy the bright, open-minded perception of children and tend to think of it as a mark of intelligence. Presumably, children who observe more will learn more.

But if the previous operating principles are true, then as a spiritual being who experiences love acutely and looks for it in all things, every child should notice just about everything. Even if the child does not tell us about it or does not let us know she has observed something, it is likely that she nevertheless has noticed it. For example, if the child witnesses a conversation between adults, she will notice the body language of the people, any emotions however subtle that they may show, what they say, and the effects of the conversation.

Because children focus on the essence of things, their impressions of a thing may differ greatly from our impression or from the impression we may want them to have. But regardless of whether we think a child's impression is correct or not, he will come to terms with it by interpreting it in the light of his previous experience and in light of his own world-view. He will take one lesson or many from any observation, and try to integrate it into his world-view. He will turn each observation and interpretation into past experience from which he can draw in the future. This turning observation into experience merely by the workings of the mind is a special skill of our species, and it goes on all the time in our children, whether they tell us about it or not.

The less understanding a child brings to an observation, the more incorrect will be her interpretation, and the more negative will be the impact on the child's world-view. It will also be more likely that she will begin to fear new experiences or observations.

One of our important jobs as parents, then, is to help our children interpret their observations. We do them no service by denying that they have observed, since the observation cannot be denied, or by fostering misinterpretation, since the essential spirituality of the child will nevertheless ultimately respond to the truth, even if it is the truth of our deception. A deceived child may respond with fear of the misunderstood thing or with distrust of the deceiving parent, but never with a few more days of "care-free youth." In other words, we can neither slow down nor speed up the detail and depth of a child's observations without disrupting his unique spiritual balance and the security of his world-view. What we can do is see that we guide our children carefully in their interpretations of what they see.

The principle of observation also means that if a child appears not to have observed something, there is a reason. If it is something significant, we should not breathe a sign of relief that it was missed but instead try to help the child articulate her interpretation of it. If it is something that we would expect to disturb the child and she does not seek our assistance in interpreting it, we should treat it as a warning that we need to improve our communication with the child.

Likewise, if the child asks some seemingly crazy question, we should not dismiss it thoughtlessly. It likely arises from some misinterpreted observation or from an on-going attempt to interpret some observation. We can take advantage of the opportunity which the child's question has offered us to participate in this process.

I shall not forget when my four-year-old son asked if any birds have four legs. In the middle of seat-belting my two-year-old daughter into the car on a day filled with errands, I was very pleased with myself when I did not answer, "Of course not, silly," with an impatience that would have said, "Don't bother me now; can't you see how busy I am?"

Instead, I said, "That would be funny, a bird with four legs. No, all birds have just two legs. They have wings where their other legs would be." I had validated the importance of a question from him and given him a bit of understanding, I thought, to add to his own observations.

His next response treated me to one of those direct exposures to the spiritual essence, the all-knowing comprehension, which is alive in every child. He said, "If the bird's legs weren't in the middle of his body but were at the back, he wouldn't stand up right—he would fall forward."

We all laughed hard together at such a funny image, a bird whose body was out of balance. But I also laughed at the wonder that the principles of physics, the laws of the universe—balance, gravity, fulcrums, whatever—were so easily observed and interpreted by a child, if merely given the room. (He enjoyed the laughing so much that he went on to say that if the legs were too far toward the front of the bird, it would fall backward.)

I do not believe my child is a budding Galileo. Or more precisely, I do not believe that he is any more a Galileo than the next child. It seems that almost any child could be a Galileo, based on his God-given gifts. Instead, this incident signified that the child had had sufficient validation of the truth of his observations and interpretations that he felt comfortable asking a strange question, continuing his train of thought, and following his perceptions where they might lead. He seemed to find it useful, fun, and rewarding (that is, validating) to observe and interpret whatever he saw.

O. P. 5

Abstraction

The child hears the most
abstract messages first

THE principle of abstraction is the most difficult of the operating principles to understand at first. But it is constantly at work in our relationships with our children. Once we can see it at work, it makes up for its conceptual difficulty. It can often make situations which seem hopelessly complex become simple and manageable.

The principle of abstraction holds that the child will pay attention first to the most abstract messages she receives from any observation, and that we can arrange the messages in a rough pattern from the most abstract and least precise down to the least abstract and most precise. In addition, the child will hear the messages in this descending order and will initially value the more abstract message as more important than the more precise message in any observation.

The most precise level is the exact physical happenings in the child's immediate vicinity at any given moment. The most abstract level is the eternal flow of cosmic energy through the universe, what we call God. In between, the levels of abstraction go from the precise to the general, from this moment to a lifetime,

21

from what we say to what we feel, from the smallest creature to God, from momentary laughter to universal love.

The child receives the cosmic message first. If it agrees with her prior experience and leaves her validated, she is free to proceed to the next level. If the message disagrees with her prior experience or leaves her invalidated, she will be stuck at that level, still seeking validation of her spiritual identity. Messages at other levels will be lost or at least distorted.

To illustrate, we can watch a baby touching his mother's skin. The baby's thoughts probably go something like this: Life is good. I love life. Then, I love mother. Then, my mother is good. Then, I like touching mother. Then, mother's skin is nice. Then, I like nice skin. Then, I like touching nice skin. Then, I would like to do this again.

Likewise, if we yell at a child for leaving his shoes around, the child will be unlikely to pay much attention to the precise message of what we say because his thoughts will go something like this: Life is pain. Mother is unhappy. Mother doesn't like me. I am no good. I hate her yelling. Mother is yelling at me. I did something wrong. I don't know how to care for my shoes. And (we hope), I shouldn't leave my shoes around.

We can always quibble about the fine lines between different levels of abstraction. But in practice, these are seldom an issue. In practice, the most important thing to remember is that if a child seems to have missed a precise message, it is probably because the child is more concerned with a message at a more abstract level. It is our job to help the child interpret the abstract message properly, so that she can move on. We will only be frustrated if we try to force the child to focus on the more precise message before she is ready.

Since none of us is perfect, we should note here that a failure to touch our children as often as they might like or an occasional bout of yelling will not by themselves leave the child on the highest level of abstraction all the time, unable to relate to his precise environment. On the contrary, the child learns by assessing and reassessing his experiences. If his prior experiences indicate that a particular message is probably wrong, he will reject it. If life is generally good, he will reject a momentary impression that it is not good, and he will be able to proceed to thoughts about the less abstract levels of meaning. But even a child with a positive world-view may be taken by surprise and be unable to respond to a precise message for a moment, because he must work through a series of negative abstract messages before he can focus on the precise one.

To continue with the yelling example, if Bobby knows generally that I love him, he will not be stuck at the level of feeling rejected by a yell, but will rather proceed on down to the level I am really yelling at—some immediate undesirable behavior. But if he does not jump to obey me immediately, I should exercise patience. It is better that I don't say, "What's wrong with you? Didn't you hear me?" Or, "What are you, stupid?" If I give him a moment, he will figure out how to take my message—that is, not personally—and will be able to respond.

On the other hand, if the child's impression so far is that life is bad, angry yelling will reinforce his impression at the highest level of abstraction, no matter how carefully we apologize, explain, and try to "make it up" to the child. In this case, either Bobby would be unable to pay attention to the precise criticism and would seek only to have the negative message overcome somehow, or he would have already come to terms with his negative world-view and would listen to the precise message, but rather than respond cooperatively to it, would look for some angle or trick to it. In any case, he would have been reconfirmed in his overall negativity.

It is worth noting here that the earlier the message, the more heavily it is weighted in the child's judgment. It is easier to change a one-year-old's perception of life and receptivity to multiple levels of observation than it is to change a three-year-old's, a ten-year-old's, or a fifteen-year-old's. But it is never too late to help someone hear positive messages. Eventually, they will be able to focus in on the precise ones too.

For the parent, awareness of the multiple levels of meaning in any interaction means that we must be as careful about how we say and do things as we are about what we say and do. Our children may pay even more attention to what seem to us like very subtle messages than they do to what we think are the most obvious ones. Messages about attitude, sense of self-worth, control over our lives, and faith in others are more likely to make a lasting impression on a child than the immediate thing we are trying to communicate.

Rather than feel self-conscious that our children are always reading our body language, we need to turn this awareness toward improving our relationship with each child. The principle of abstraction means that when we have been dragged in over our heads by some precise problem, we can let it go. It is more important that our child see that we can regain our perspective on the situation than that we force our position on having a washed face, a helping of vegetables, or whatever may be the precise problem. It also means that we can dispense with guilt about not knowing every precise thing which we want our children to learn. If we parents give the right messages at the abstract level, the child will seek the precise knowledge she needs. If we share the knowledge and skills that we have, the child will feel validated and have the strength to seek out the knowledge and skills she needs.

The principle of abstraction can help us dispense with most kinds of parental guilt. Guilt is perhaps the single most counterproductive emotion most parents can feel. Although anger and even hate will eventually pass, the guilt that they leave behind makes future outbreaks more likely and clouds over the genuineness and candor of our later interactions. If we realize that something we have done has given a message we did not intend, we can correct that impression or counteract it at the next opportunity, even though we can never undo or replay the scene that gave rise to the negative message. Unlike precise situations, which are never exactly the same again, abstract messages of the same sort come up all the time. We can dispense with guilt about a single incident, because we can be confident that we will soon have another opportunity to correct an incorrect abstract message. We can even create an opportunity from almost any situation.

For example, suppose we forbid Marisa to play in the rain on a warm summer night, but for one reason or another, we neglect to do it gently with an offering of some persuasive reasons. We act angry and impatient. The child may first feel that we don't want her to have any fun, that we don't love her. She may never get to thinking about wet hair in the bed, mud on the floor, or whatever is our real concern. If we see the disappointment or realize that we did not really have a genuine concern in mind to support our negative response, we may feel very guilty. But we may see no way to correct the error. We may be afraid to change our minds. "We can't let her think she can get her way just by looking sad!"

But the abstraction principle may help us decide which concern should dictate our actions. Which is more abstract: the message that we will be stubborn because we fear that our authority has been threatened, or the message that being sad will bring sympathy? The first relates directly to one's self-esteem and will have more weight with the child. The second relates only to how to get one's way in a precise situation and will have less weight. In addition, the first message is one we would rather not communicate, because we would rather our child did not adopt a defensive or authoritative attitude toward others. The second, in contrast, may be less harmful. After all, human beings are able to communicate sadness by mere facial expression probably exactly because we have the unique power to respond positively to each other's facial expressions. Her sad expression tells us how strongly she feels about the matter and suggests that we should make an extra effort to find a compromise between her desires and ours.

The principle of abstraction, then, allows us to back off and to change our minds, without the guilt that we have appeared weak, wishy-washy, or unthinking. We may find that it feels very good to say, "Oh, well, I didn't know you wanted to do it so much. I just thought it would be a bother, but there is really no strong reason not to."

If on the other hand we choose not to back off, it can also be done without guilt, if we act according to the principle of abstraction. We might be tempted to these guilt feelings: "Why am I so mean?" "Why can't I let her have any fun?" "I'll have to make it up to her—I'll play outside with her tomorrow, or I'll buy her some cookies."

But if we act according to the abstraction principle, we will see that we need not somehow "make it up to her," compensate favor for missed favor, or give double indulgence for mistakenly denied indulgence. We can offer validation at a higher level. The next time she asks to do something which seems to be a bit of a hassle but not that bad, something like playing outside in the drizzle, we can remember, and say "Yes, OK."

Or, we could even just tell her how we feel about the incident, when our thoughts have settled down. Most likely, she will accept our thinking as a validating apology for the way we handled the matter and forgive us immediately. We may find ourselves wondering what all our internal turmoil was about.

If we are used to standing our precise ground no matter what the abstract implications, or insisting on immediate precise responses rather than accepting a certain ebb and flow in the parent-child relationship, there may be a bit of adjustment for both parent and child before either can hear and accept the real messages. But the child is ready to hear.

If it rains all day on your first day in Paris, you will carry an umbrella the next day. If it doesn't rain the next day, you may still carry your umbrella. But after three or four days of clear skies, you will probably change your impression of Paris, and leave your umbrella behind. So go the adjustments parents and children make when they learn to deal with the most abstract first.

Referencing

The child may need referencing
to a different level

OURS is clearly a complex world. A child's world is constantly expanding. If new observations come too fast, if interpretations conflict, or if messages on different levels disagree, the child's behavior will reflect the stress. In addition to helping the child interpret what he sees at the level at which he is observing, the situation may need referencing to a different level of meaning. The principle of referencing functions closely with the validation and abstraction principles. If something is troubling the child, he will not be receptive to guidance unless we first guide him by reference to a higher, presumably more positive level of abstraction.

For example, if dinner guests have occupied most of the evening, as well as a day of preparations, Georgette may get extremely cranky just before dinner is served. "How could you be so nice all day and so horrible right now, at the worst time?" we may think and even say. But the child is feeling, "This is the last straw. All day I've been on my own; now I will not have their attention for all of dinner too. They really don't care about me after all. I'm worthless, disintegrated, in pain!" Rattling the dinner chairs is the least she can do to express her pain. We might yell or whisper dramatically about how troublesome and inconvenient this behavior is. But that would be reinforcing the pain and the negative world-view. Instead, we can reference the situation to a higher level. We can let her know that her needs matter and that we love her, despite the opposite impression which the temporary neglect of this evening gives. With the reference to familiar validating levels, the child will be most likely to quickly abandon the objectionable behavior and be cooperative and cheerful once more.

As this example shows, referencing is the specific device for helping the child interpret conflicts between messages on different levels. Yes, we are putting off the child temporarily because we are preoccupied with our guests. But no, this does not mean that we do not care. The rejection is only at the precise level of tonight in the context of the party. It does not refer to anything more abstract. At the higher level of abstraction, all is just as she thought. We love her, and we will play with her tomorrow, and we would be especially happy if she would take part in enjoying our friends with us tonight.

It is important to note here that telling her all these things is not as good as demonstrating them. If what we say conflicts with what we do, the child will be more impressed by the latter. Also, any assertion implies that the opposite is possible. Thus, if the child is concerned that we don't love her, saying we do does not totally overcome the fear. She may feel that we have confirmed that it may be an issue. It is better to save the direct assertions of love for times when it is not an issue.

By the same token, promises of future behavior will carry little weight. The child lives now and is not easily impressed by promises of future love. Also, it may appear to a child in a negative frame of mind that promises are evidence of guilt on our part, confirming her fears that we may not love her.

Rather than assertions and promises, validating action is the best solution. Five minutes of focused attention will most likely adequately reference the situation. Totally focused attention, no matter for how short a time, will go far to demonstrate that all is right with the child's world. It will help the child put the evening in the perspective of her normal or prior experience.

Some effective ways to reference the situation are: We can tell her about what a help she has been in preparing the party and how we appreciate it. We can choose some common, joyful activity that reminds her of past validating experiences and spend a few minutes together on it, like reading a favorite book. We can seek the child's help with tearing lettuce for the salad or arranging bread on a dish. We can step off our busy pedestal and do something silly, so that we can laugh and hug together for a moment. Or we can call on our spouse to do one of these.

Whatever we choose to do, we will have lifted the child away from the negative message she received at the precise level of a temporary, unusual situation toward the more abstract level of a happy home which all the family wants to share with friends.

It is often difficult to remember that a child may need referencing. We are often trapped even more easily than our child into the least abstract levels of everyday life. It is remarkable that we could imagine ourselves victimized by our children, for instance, when they distract us from our precise task at hand. If we recognize the higher level of abstraction, we will quickly see that we have complete control of the situation. We need only acknowledge the child at an appropriate level of meaning, and we both will feel renewed.

Allowance

The child thrives on allowance
rather than force

THE life force in children inspires their growth and development. Every child is a unique individual. We cannot force our children to grow or develop at any preconceived rate or in any particular direction. If we thrust patterns of behavior upon them before they are ready, they will hear the wrong message, learn the wrong lesson. They may learn the pattern and adopt it to please us, but they will have learned in addition that they should not rely on their own timing, motivation, and instincts to yield good results. After they are on their own, without our pressure on them, they will not have these to rely on, because they will long since have been abandoned in disuse.

Timing is a recurrent theme in joyful parenting. We are so concerned with transmitting substantive learning and precise skills to our children that we often ignore that the timing of various behaviors and skills plays a large role in our children's lives, as it does in ours. Something said in a moment of tension may elicit an unwanted response or even go unheeded, for example, while the same thing said at a light-hearted time will be understood as we intended it, that is, at its appropriate level of meaning.

Timing can make the difference between whether we laugh at a joke, whether we get the job we want, or whether we accept a marriage proposal. It is just as important—perhaps even more so—in raising children. Each of the various stages that children go through will yield different messages on the abstract level, depending upon whether we try to introduce those stages when we think it is time or when the child indicates that it is time. Some of these stages are: learning to use the toilet, feeding oneself, reading, saying please and thank you, and playing the piano. We will look closely at some of these in Part II.

In each case, if the parent makes a choice that the child is capable of making, the child will hear a message that the parent does not trust her, that she is therefore not trustworthy, and that she should not rely on her own judgment in the future. If we do not allow the child to develop her own sense of timing, we may find that the child will not have the advantage of the kind of "luck" that will put her in the right place at the right time, will make people laugh at her jokes, will get her the job she wants, or will free her to recognize the right marriage proposal at the right time.

Of course we must keep in mind that a temporary slip on our part will not destroy a child's self-esteem. But we need to be aware that the child will hear any message. He will disregard it if it is inconsistent with the weight of his prior experience. But if it should become part of a pattern of similar messages, self-esteem will gradually diminish. The child's ability to make decisions at appropriate times will stagnate, and a child who appeared headed toward independence may suddenly stop his progress.

Aside from the direct message that the child may not be trustworthy, additional messages come through, because of the tensions of the situation. If we try to teach a behavior that the child is not ready to learn, the child may resist, lose interest, feel frustrated with failure, feel inadequate for disliking something she is supposed to like, or feel denial of some activity she does want. We may well respond to any of these reactions with our own sense of frustration, impatience, or anger. These compound the initial negative message about timing and judgment and may cause the child to associate unpleasantness with the behavior we are trying to teach. The child may then not be interested in the behavior even when the time comes that she would otherwise have been ready for it.

For the parent, the principle of allowance removes unnecessary burdens. For example, we do not bear the burden of turning a savage creature into a thoughtful human being. The child will not be a heartless, ill-mannered person, if we do not beat good manners and thoughtfulness into him. There is no need for us even to entertain the idea of forced learning, which in the abstract embarrasses most parents anyhow. If our overall message is sound, and we provide a stimulating environment and a good example, the child will not only develop appropriate interests and activities, he will also learn decision-making skills and self-confidence.

On the other hand, the principle of allowance demands a much closer relationship with the child than does forced learning, because we need to be promptly sensitive to his developmental needs and interests as they surface. We need to read our children's signals, take our cues from our children, listen to what our children say.

Of course after we get the first cue about a particular interest, we cannot immediately stop listening. If the child puts on her own shirt one morning, we must not overreact: "Oh, good! Now she will start dressing herself, finally!" Instead, we must approach each development on a more abstract level. What we have is an opportunity to help the child feel good about dressing herself. Compliments or, even better, nonjudgmental sharing and empathy for the child's feelings are the most constructive responses we can give: "Isn't that fun, that you put on your shirt for yourself, just like I do!" An exaggerated expectation that all of a sudden this will be the regular pattern of dressing is most likely to backfire and put off that new stage. The child will fear that our over-reaction means they have gone too far, and they may well back off from the new challenge. They may also regret giving up the extra moment of closeness which having a parent dress them gives, if we suddenly treat them differently because of this new development.

Instead of pushing ahead, we must continue listening to our child, encouraging each new activity not because that is just what we wanted him to do, but because that is just what the child wants to do. Allowance means we try hard to open up opportunities for our children, to expose them to the richness of life, and to broaden their observations, so that they can appreciate their own potential. We avoid prejudging what direction and timing they will follow. Instead we allow them to make their own informed choices, by supporting them spiritually with our attentive guidance and love.

This approach frees us parents from the duty to control our child's every move and from the feeling that we will be judged by the way our children behave. It frees us for the joy of watching our children unfold like butterflies emerging from their cocoons before our eyes. We will feel only joy at the wonderful array of colors which will appear. If we have not prejudged what colors they should be or tried to impose our will in order to produce the colors we wanted, there can be no disappointment to interfere with our joy.

Trust

We can trust that we
and our children
have what we need

THE operating principle of trust works closely with the principle of allowance. We will feel comfortable allowing a child to go at her own speed only if we feel that we can trust the child's own energy, desire to learn, and sense of timing to keep her moving in the direction which is best for the child.

Our sense of trust in our child can begin immediately. If the parents are with the baby immediately after birth, they will have their first opportunity to observe the trustworthiness of the healthy newborn. When the baby has a need, she is quick to communicate it. A hungry, cold, hot, or lonely baby will yell so that no one can miss it.

This first impression of trustworthiness may be reason alone to oppose the separation of parents from their newborn baby in the hospital. Some well-meaning nurses give nonessential excuses for separation, such as the baby takes a lot of care right away, the mother needs to rest, the mother is too unfamiliar with mothering routines to do them round the clock, or the baby's crying is too much for the tired mother. These excuses give the parent the impression that the baby's needs are hard to anticipate, hard to meet, virtually unending, and perhaps even unreasonable. This first impression is an unfortunate one and an inaccurate one. Sadly, it can stick with us for the next twenty years. We may never learn to trust our child to communicate her needs.

But we can let our trust grow if we keep that early bonding period simple. We can keep the family together. We can seek all the help we want from hospital personnel, but we can stay in control of the situation. We can allow our communication with the baby to develop, so that we can understand when he seeks our help.

I will not forget nursing my first child for the first time shortly after birth. I was a bit unsure of myself. I was thinking, "How do I do it? How will he know what to do? Won't he be terribly frustrated if I don't do it properly the first time?"

But what I received, right in the middle of all these worries, was a giant lesson in trust. The baby clamped on and sucked as if his life depended on it. (It did, of course, as far as the baby could know.) I realized right then that I could trust my child to see that he was fed, so long as I made myself available. If a child half an hour old could make a full-grown woman jump with the power of his tiny jaws to satisfy his hunger, I should pay close attention to his expressions of his needs. These should go far in helping to determine how best to care for him.

Of course many babies don't latch on to the breast right away. But in the vast majority of cases, they will when they are ready and given the opportunity.

It may seem easy to trust a baby to let us know when she is hungry or too hot or bored, but more difficult to rely on the child's cues as far as toilet training, moving into her own bed, going to school, learning to read, or cutting her own carrot sticks. Hunger is a basic need essential to survival. These other behaviors are merely cultural patterns, not necessarily essential to life. We may wonder if we can trust that the child will seek to adopt these behaviors without our active intervention.

The principle of trust tells us that our child has what he needs. He has the desire to do what he observes that others around him are doing. While any particular cultural pattern may not be essential to life in today's world, it has been essential to life for ninety-nine percent of the history of humanity that a child adopt the cultural pattern of those around him. The cultural pattern gave the child the behaviors he needed to survive in his immediate environment and to be accepted by his immediate human community. If the child were to resist learning the language of those around him, was not inclined toward their habits of hygiene, or did not adopt their modes of eating, he would not survive.

From this history we can assume that we can trust our child to want to adopt behavior patterns which are favorable to her survival in the community. The child will tend to be ready, willing, and able to adopt the behavior patterns of those around her.

For example, we tend to assume that our children should be in school by at least age six and preferably earlier. But there is nothing essential to a child which requires a school experience at any of these ages. Our child gets exposed to the idea through friends and siblings and soon becomes eager to participate, even though the experience is largely a great unknown to the child.

However, if we do not expose our child to the behavior patterns of older children or adults, she is unlikely to want to follow these patterns on her own, even if we tell her that it is for her own good. For example, if the child never sees another person use the toilet, her motivation will be minimal to use it herself, and she may even imagine there is something wrong with her when we seek to have her use it. If the child never sees his parents go to sleep or wake up, his own patterns are not as secure, selected as they are from a myriad of possible human patterns. Similarly, if the child never observes cooperative, loving resolution of disagreements, he will have little understanding of how to go about it, and we can place little trust in his ability to resolve disagreements on his own. If we want our child to be self-motivated, then, so that we can trust him to let his needs and wants be known and to take appropriate steps toward getting what he needs or wants, we must be careful to allow a comfortable exposure to our own culture's patterns. When the child can observe the norms of the family, the community, the country, and human society in general, he will want to take part.

The principle of trust gives important comfort to the parent who wonders when and how to introduce all the troubles of the world: death, crime, war, famine, alcohol and drug abuse, sexual perversion, and more. Because we want to raise a responsible community-minded adult, we know we cannot hide these things. On the other hand, we don't want to shatter a positive world-view, shock the child into nightmares, stimulate misplaced fascination, or paralyze the child with fear or hopelessness.

The best solution seems to be to share one's own public life and concerns, let the child observe how we approach them, and stay close enough that we can interpret all along—before, during, and after observations. For example, if we go to a meeting about water pollution, we can answer the child's question about what we are doing. But we need not try to expound upon the threat of general ground-water contamination, unless the child asks that question.

Similarly, if the child happens to see a newsreel about a violent revolution, we can help her interpret the observation. We need not try to read the child's mind. Rather, we can bring out our own most basic reactions and share them aloud. "That's terrible. I don't like it when people fight and kill each other," we might say. Often the child will ask "Why?" But if not, she may still be sufficiently impressed by what she saw that our guidance will help integrate the observation into her expanding world-view with the least harm.

We must be careful not to offer gratuitous information, or the child may become uncomfortable that we will turn everything into a lesson. Rather, we can address ourselves to feelings. If the child does not respond to our first remark, but we suspect the observation needs some interpreting, we can say, "Sometimes I wonder why they do it." Answering our own question may seem strange, but the child can listen without being on the spot. "Sometimes people fight each other because they blame each other for terrible problems in their lives. Some people in other parts of the world have many sad problems, like not enough food or too few houses."

If we still elicit no response from the child, we can let the matter go, knowing that we have made ourselves open to helping with any concerns that she may have. Then we must stay alert to any indications that the child still needs help with her interpretation. The matter may come up the next day or even a week or more later. If we make ourselves open and available, we can trust that our child will eventually ask questions until she is satisfied. When her understanding becomes more sophisticated, the matter may well come up again, and then again.

Another important aspect of trust affects how we treat mistakes. If the child makes a mistake, we can do one of three things. We can reject it: "What's wrong with you? My boy doesn't do that!" We can tolerate it, thinking that we can teach him how to do it right: "No, Johnny, that's not right. Here's how. Do it over again. Next time you'll get it right the first time." Or we can accept it, and trust the child to learn on his own by his mistake, while we focus our guidance at the most abstract levels, unless he actually seeks our help in correcting the mistake: "You worked really hard at that. That must have been fun. The M is upside down, but that's all right. Very good!" If the child says, "How do you make the M right?" then and only then would we tell him.

At the higher level of abstraction, the first reaction tells the child that he can't be trusted. He does not live up to expectations. The second reaction is not so negative. But the child may still sense failure and inadequacy. Doing it over again is a bit like putting a dog's nose to his mistake. Because our great advantage over dogs and other creatures is our phenomenal ability to learn merely by envisioning experiences without ever living them, such crude teaching is unnecessary.

The third reaction demonstrates our trust that the child will progress under his own power. If he has made a mistake, he will learn by it for next time. We need only let the child see his error. We need not attach any special importance to it or let it overshadow the child's accomplishment or his joy in the effort that he has made.

Popular wisdom might say that this reaction is deceptive. We are setting the child up with praise, only to tear him down by pointing out a mistake. But this impression of the situation stems from our own upbringing, not from the situation itself. Most of us were taught that mistakes were terrible things. But if sinners are to be forgiven, it is so that they can learn from their mistakes. As a star in the new field of personal computers said recently when his meteoric company suddenly failed because of poor management: "You've got to fail some of the time or you aren't trying hard enough. . . . You cannot be the kind of person who takes failure hard and be an entrepreneur."

We can teach our children to minimize the disappointment of a mistake, maximize successes, and get on with learning by communicating to them the trust we place in them. If children mature by internalizing the values of early authority figures, self-esteem is most likely to thrive in those whose parents treated them with esteem when they were children. Only with practice can we become comfortable with giving praise and minimizing mistakes. But the rewards will quickly become apparent.

The principle of trust does not relieve parents of any real responsibilities. It does relieve us of a host of worries and imagined burdens which can be overwhelming. It also suggests how we can fulfill our responsibilities more consciously and effectively. If we respect our children and allow them to contribute their own energies to their up-bringing, our mutual trust will grow steadily.

Guidance

We need only guide our children,
not control them

OUR role as parents is to guide our children, not to control them. We often hear new parents marvel that a baby "already has a mind of her own." As the other principles suggest, from the start the baby wants to reach out, relate to her environment, and reinforce her world-view that being born was a good thing. A child will not willingly choose to do something she knows is harmful unless her positive world-view has been injured. We do not then need to feel that we are always fighting to control a contrary force. Rather, we are seeking to guide an agreeable but inexperienced force.

As parents, we should inform our child of any dangers in his environment and protect him from any dangers which are too sophisticated for him to appreciate. But if we go any further in our control over the child, either mentally or physically, we risk interfering with the child's sense of personal competence to deal with the world around him. We also close out many opportunities for learning about that world.

For example, a common situation involves a child's wish to do something which the parent doesn't want him to do. Often, if we took the time to think it through, we would find that we are against the project for reasons unrelated to the child. Perhaps the project will make a mess which we don't want to have to clean up. Perhaps we see the possibility of some harm to the child, and we know we can avert it with careful attention but we don't want to take the time. Or we had other plans for what to do during this half hour which did not include supervision of an original project. In any case, we say, "No."

If the child cannot see the danger or the risk, she is likely to go through these thoughts: "Life is bad, I can't do what I want. Daddy doesn't love me, because he says no for no reason. I am no good, because I chose to do something Daddy thinks is bad. I can't be trusted to make good decisions."

If the situation is not too common in the child's experience, she will be able to reject all these incorrect abstract thoughts and continue to the more precise immediate point. "Daddy usually says yes. He must have a reason for saying no. He is too busy now to tell me his reason."

The principle of guidance means that a child will thrive best if we concern ourselves with how to steer our child around any obstacle to accomplishing her desired activity, rather than with whether the activity should be prohibited altogether.

Often the situation will require us to draw the boundaries of permissible behavior. For example, we will not let the child play in the street because of the obvious hazards. Though the dangers of fast-moving cars are obvious to us, a young child with no experience of injury, car crashes, or death may not appreciate the risk, and we must establish a clear boundary. We draw a mental boundary on this side of the forbidden activity and have no qualms about saying, "Absolutely not."

At the other extreme, we would be overbearing if we were to forbid the child to play outside because he might conceivably be drawn to the street. We are comfortable saying yes to playing outside, because we know that we can protect the child adequately by checking out the window occasionally to be sure that he is a safe distance from the street.

Between activities that we generally prohibit and activities that we generally permit are a seemingly huge number of activities which we will permit or prohibit depending on the time and circumstances. Each of these can either build the child's confidence and capabilities or detract from them, depending upon our attitude and how we say yes or no.

For instance, if we forbid the child to play ball, because the ball may go into the street and draw him after it, we may be drawing an artificial boundary, too close to the child and too far from the real danger. Is playing ball dangerous? Certainly we would want to explain why we think it is dangerous in these circumstances. But even then the child will still wonder why we cannot trust him to keep the ball out of the street or to leave it in the street until he sought our help to retrieve it. The child may respond, "But I can keep it out of the street."

By drawing the boundary too close to the child, we have set ourselves up to reinforce the child's negative impression of our faith in him. If we say, "No, you won't be able to keep it out of the street," or "I still say no," we will be reinforcing the negative message. The child will hear one of these negative messages: that we believe the child is a poor judge of what he is able to do, that we gave a fake reason in the first place, or that we are merely being arbitrary with our rules, which is tantamount to not caring about the needs or wants of the ruled.

We put ourselves in this trap by overcontrolling the child's behavior, merely because we know more than he does. Because we know that children easily get excited playing ball, we know that the ball will sooner or later go into the street. But the child cannot be expected to know this if he has not yet played much ball, and it is not our place to tell him that he has any limitations. Instead, we must draw our line of prohibition as close as we can to the absolutely necessary one, in order to give the child the room to learn his own limitations, while maintaining and developing confidence in his personal judgment.

In the ball-playing situation, probably the best way to handle the situation would be to ask the child to try to keep the ball from going into the street and instruct him that if the ball does go in the street, he must not follow it but must get our help.

With this approach, we have kept our abstract messages accurate and preserved the child's self-esteem. In addition, by not predicting that the child will fail to keep the ball out of the street, we have actually enhanced his self-esteem. We have left him the room to learn one more thing about himself and his environment, without feeling badly about it. Without our giving a patronizing message about our opinion of the child's abilities, the child is free to accept, based on his new experience, that it is almost impossible to keep balls forever out of the street.

We may ask ourselves, though, will he remember not to follow the ball? If we are uncomfortable with the risks of trusting the child in a potentially dangerous situation, we should not push ourselves to it. Rather, we should take on still more work. We should undertake to check the child frequently, without his knowing that we are checking, until we have overcome our fears and confirmed that our trust is well-placed.

If we cannot overcome our fears in this way, then chances are that we do have a real fear, and that we should draw a more narrow boundary. We can then explain to the child that because of the serious dangers, we will feel comfortable only if we are watching when he plays ball. As long as we make ourselves available to watch reasonably often, this will have minimal impact on the child. Also, we have still avoided saying that the child could not handle the situation. It is the serious consequences of any failure, not the likelihood of one, that has caused us to limit the activity. The child need not feel that any inadequacy of his caused the limitation.

It is important, then, that we avoid limiting our children by our own fears. We must deal with our own fears first, before we limit the child. We need not be impatient with ourselves for an immediate answer if we need a few minutes to consider a child's request. A child is surprisingly patient while we take time to consider our response to his thoughts. In contrast, if in our haste we create limits which are artificial, the child will sense their artificiality and resent us and himself for his limitations. He may also decide that the world is full of arbitrary rules and may lose the sense of control over his own destiny which he will need to be most effective in adult life.

While drawing lines carefully seems more work for parents—more talking, more thinking, more quiet watching— in the long run, it is far less taxing. We will have fostered a child who trusts himself to know his own limits and who will seek us out for guidance whenever he is in a new situation with unknown risks. We will not have to watch over his shoulder all his life, because the child will have learned when to call for help.

Though emotional risks may seem more difficult in some ways, they come under this principle just as physical risks do. For example, if we want to forbid our children from dating when all their friends are dating and when the children want to, we must check our fears before we set artificial limits. We must ask ourselves these questions: Are our fears real? If so, can the desired activity be refined in such a way as to satisfy our fears without prohibiting the activity outright? If not, how can we present our reasons in a way which does not belittle the child or suggest that we do not trust her judgment or sense of timing?

In the dating situation, we may well be able to satisfy our fears by limiting the number of outings, the number of people involved, the late hours, or the destination. If these will not do, we must not only share our concerns with the child, but we must help her understand how she is different from her friends, without belittling her or her friends. We could say that her friends' parents don't care or don't know what's good for their children or that their friends are bad influences. But all these carry negative abstract messages. Rather, we should affirm the free choice of each of us and say that other parents are free to do as they choose, that this is the way we choose to protect our child, and that at this stage in her life our family prefers to put more emphasis on study and friendship than on dating and romance. Though this may seem artificial at first, children will often respond surprisingly positively to a frank assertion of well-considered choices which we have made for our family. While they may still rankle at the precise denial, they will still feel good about the effort we put into the decision and the fact that we value family solidarity and consistency. Still, if at all possible, we should reach some compromise which gives the child as much freedom as we can teach ourselves to be comfortable with.

Overprotection may protect our children from emotional threats from outside, but it leaves them wide open to emotional threats from within. If we set reasonable, well-founded limits as often as we can, our children will sense our confidence in them, will internalize it, and will not be ashamed to seek help when they sense a dangerous situation which they may not be able to handle. Children will always seek to escape the control of a parent. But they will take comfort in the availability of guidance, as opposed to control. Ideally they will see that as they grow, ever fewer situations will involve parental control and ever more situations will involve our guidance only. This progression promises a parent-child relationship which will bring joy even when the child is an independent adult.

Expectation

Children seek to please but tend to fulfill expectations

CHILDREN generally want to please their parents. When we express our desires, our children will generally want to conform to them. But they are able to receive messages at numerous levels of meaning. They not only hear what we say, they also detect what we expect of them from the way we speak, from our tone, our body language, and our choice of words. Because they listen to the abstract messages as well as the precise ones and tend to give the abstract ones more weight, they will more often meet our expectations than our expressed desires.

This principle explains how, despite their strong desire to please, our children often seem perverse, obstinate, and disagreeable. They behave this way when they face what they perceive as a conflict between what we say we want and what we actually expect of them. If we challenge a child to overcome our disbelief or if we threaten him by withholding our approval or pleasure until he has performed some precise behavior, we have communicated negative messages, even if only momentarily. The child may hear that we do not trust him to know what he is capable of. Or he may hear that we are not pleased with him as a whole. A child will be more concerned with this distrust and displeasure at the abstract levels than with the precise request. He will have a hard time addressing the precise request with a positive attitude, since he senses rejection at the higher levels.

To illustrate, suppose we say, "Please don't get your dress dirty, Betsy," as we send her out the door to the back yard. Betsy will hear at least three things. First she hears that there is a possibility or even a likelihood that the dress will get dirty. We "have put the idea into her head." Second, she hears that we expect that she may well get it dirty. Third, she hears that we don't want it to get dirty. The first and second messages are more abstract than the third. The child will screen these first then, even though the third is the only one we meant to communicate.

The first message tells her about her world: Dresses can get dirty. The second tells her about herself. We expect that she may dirty her dress, and since we are usually right, she may well dirty her dress. If these two messages hurt the child's self-image, the third is unlikely to get through.

Even if it does get through, the nagging lack of confidence we have instilled by the second message may turn our fear that the dress will get dirty into a self-fulfilling prophecy. The child's preoccupation with and self-consciousness about keeping the dress clean to please us or to foil our negative expectations may well make the child clumsier and more awkward than she would otherwise be. Betsy will be more prone to accidents if she is watching herself this way, and we may well end up with a dirty dress.

This kind of self-fulfilling expectation can have the vicious effect of decreasing further our confidence in our child, so that at the next opportunity, we may communicate even greater lack of trust and pleasure. If we cannot break out of this downward spiral, we may facilitate the very incompetence and clumsiness which we sought to prevent.

We must be careful, then, to think before we speak and to say exactly what we mean when we are communicating our desires to our children. It may seem cumbersome at first, but the extra effort is well worthwhile. With some conscious practice, we can learn to think instantly in terms that will communicate our desires to our children and give them the information they need to gear their behavior toward fulfilling those desires without giving any negative messages. In the case of Betsy's dress, we could say: "It is easy to slip in the grass when it has dew on it like this morning. I would really like to have your dress neat and clean when the guests come. Could you be especially careful to keep it clean?" We have shown our appreciation that she generally is careful. We have given our reason for mentioning the issue this time. The child is secure and can respond directly to the precise message that she should take special care this time to keep the dress clean.

Because we can sense that our child wants to please us, sometimes we find ourselves trying to manipulate the child to our momentary advantage by pleading with him. For example, I might say to Mike, "Won't you please clean up your room, just for me?" This kind of pleading has an amazing variety of messages, mostly negative.

These are some of the negative thoughts which pleading may stimulate:

PARENT: "I can't trust you to do what is right, just because it is right."

CHILD: "I am untrustworthy."

PARENT: "You should do something because someone else wants it, not because you want it or because it is right."

CHILD: "Virtue is not its own reward. My wants and needs aren't important."

PARENT: "I assume that you will not clean up."

CHILD: "Why should I clean up if she has already prejudged me as a slob?"

PARENT: "I offer myself (my desires) as a reason of last resort."

CHILD: "Personal wants come last in value."

PARENT: "I am begging you. I feel ineffective as a person."

CHILD: "She doesn't think much of herself. I must be worth even less."

If this sounds too pessimistic, we must keep in mind that while the child may not hear them all, any one of these thoughts is too many if it is incorrect. While there is nothing wrong with negative information if it is accurate, we do not want to communicate inaccurate negative information when it could be harmful to our child.

With all these possible negative messages, it is extremely rare that pleading gets the desired response without leaving some wounds. In this example, only if Mike was a very confident, mature child could he respond positively. For him, this kind of parental pleading will have been rare, and the child will be able to focus on my precise message, because he is able to grasp the abstract message that I am the one feeling desperate and in need of positive validation. Cleaning up his room in that case would be a way of saying, "Hey, Mom, you're OK. I do care how you feel. Just because you want it, I'll do it." This would be an example of the rewards of joyful parenting. Children who sense they have pleased their parents all along will take pleasure in a mutually supportive relationship and walk the extra mile for us when we need nurturing and validation. But we cannot expect this kind of behavior from a very young child or from any child who is not presently very well validated.

If the child is not old enough or secure enough to overcome the negative messages, pleading will be useless, and in fact it can make a parent feel even more helpless. If the pleading fails, I have no more tricks, because I have revealed my low self-esteem and have no more power over my situation. My only way out is to let go of my error and begin to apply the operating principles again. I can accept that this is a bad time, keep faith that good times will return, allow the child some room while I collect myself, and then share with the child some of this validation which I, as the more mature of us, can give to myself.

A better approach than pleading would be any of the following, even assuming that we have already had a long argument on the issue.

"All right, you don't want to clean up your room now. I feel terrible when the house is such a mess. Could you just clear the cars off the floor today?"

"Maybe we can do it together."

"How about after you play outside or after dinner?"

These responses acknowledge the importance of the child's desires. They still communicate our wishes. They also set a good example of effective behavior: We have made a constructive suggestion, even in a tense moment of apparent conflict.

The desire to please is an inborn mechanism to help the human baby learn all that she can from her parents. It is essential for the safety of the individual child, because doing what her parents want may save her from death or injury. It is also essential for the survival of the human species, because doing what her parents want means adopting various habits and patterns of behavior which her particular culture has found most useful in its particular environment.

To take advantage of the desire to please in order to manipulate the child when we want to impose our own momentary will on her cannot only damage the child's positive view of herself, it may also hamper her overall ability to learn. Whenever she feels herself in a situation in which she can please or not please someone, she will feel a sense of conflict, because in her past experience, pleasing someone else has been associated with negative feelings about herself. Not pleasing someone else or resisting fulfilling someone else's expectations becomes, then, a desperate way of asserting one's identity. A child who has adopted these patterns is very difficult to teach, let alone to live with and love.

But knowing that the desire to please is a special trait and that a child will tend to fill our expectations, parents can discover new ways to help children grow toward maturity and a joyful life. First of all, we can try to avoid any negative expectations of our children. Then if we do have some, we should keep them to ourselves, especially after the fact. We should avoid saying, "I knew you couldn't do it," or "I thought so." Then, if we have controlled our negative expectations, we can work on developing positive ones. These should not be precise ambitions or high standards of achievement, though. Those are almost as dangerous as negative expectations, because the child feels so inadequate when he fails to please. And even if he does achieve and fulfill the ambitions of his parents, he may find out later that what pleased his parents does not necessarily please him. A doctor may find out late in his career that he became a doctor not to please himself but to please his parents and that he would rather have been a zoologist, an entrepreneur, or an artist.

Rather than lay out a future for our child, whether it be negative or positive in our view, we need to focus our expectations at the highest levels, where they will do the most good in validating the child. We must expect, simply, that the spiritual essence of the child will shine through and manifest itself in everything the child does.

Next, we can use the child's desire to please us as a wonderful means to offer validation of this essence whenever we can. We can express our particular pleasure at the child's best efforts. But we can also express our general pleasure at having the child near us, at sharing experiences with her, at seeing what she chooses to wear or to eat or to draw or to read, and at talking, laughing, or playing with the child.

We all know that the simplest of compliments gives anyone a feeling of self-worth. Children respond to these, too. If a parent can't think of anything which pleases him at a given moment, even a statement like "You sure can yell loud," can be validating and break the tension, so long as the body language and tone show that the parent is not criticizing but is actually enjoying the achievement—that is, seeing the bright side of the situation.

As parents we also can help our children interpret the expectations of others, so that they understand that only they can make the decisions that will govern their lives, and that others' expectations must be taken only as suggestions at best. Well validated children will need no outside standards to stimulate their efforts or to help them evaluate their performance. They will aim to feel their own progress and to please themselves. If we have kept our expectations at the spiritual level, their efforts and performance will please us, too.

O. P. 11

Receptivity

The child is receptive to
genuine communication

OUR children are receptive to genuine communication. As the preceding principles indicate, they will not tolerate falsehood or hypocrisy. But they will eventually respond to genuine messages which tend to validate their spiritual identity. If we treat them with respect, they will listen to what we say.

Childhood receptivity is closely related to the desire to please and the sensitivity to others' expectations. All these qualities derive from the tendency of children to grasp the essence of any observation or experience. All serve the special human purpose of learning. These innate qualities make children uniquely responsive to information and cues from their environment and from us, their parents.

For us, this principle means that we have a great deal of control over the responses we elicit from our child. If we are able to keep in mind the other principles, especially referencing and trust, we will seldom if ever see a need to punish a child. The accepted purposes of punishment in the adult world are three: revenge, removal, and rehabilitation. We need to consider each of these.

Few of us believe in revenge against a child, if we tolerate it at all. But we should be aware that revenge can briefly control our behavior. If we feel that our child has spoiled a visit with a friend, for example, we may just feel like denying him something he wants later. We may kid ourselves that there is some learning experience in the trade, but some broad lesson like the generalization that bad behavior will bring bad results will be lost on a child who will instead be occupied with the double injury of having displeased us and having us deny his wants. Learning can proceed only when the child's basic identity is secure. When we suddenly shift our thinking into a teaching mode in the middle of a punishment, we should check that we are not merely rationalizing a desire for revenge.

Revenge can also lead to harsher punishment than we intended. Often we resent in our children the feelings of anger and helplessness that their defiant or rebellious behavior stimulates in us. These feelings usually have more to do with our own childhood than with our children. If these feelings get the best of us, punishment is most destructive to the child and is best abandoned entirely. Meanwhile we need to deal with our feelings, often most effectively through a local self-help group.

Removal can be a legitimate purpose of punishment, but it need only be a last resort. An occasion for removal may arise when the actors in a situation are so inextricably interwined in their negative messages that removing one of the actors is the only way to reestablish order and perspective. Hence the occasional need to ask the child to leave the room or to sit on the stairs for a few minutes. Even this kind of response should be handled with care. If we force any more removal than necessary, the child will sense that there is revenge at the base of the action and will resent the injustice. Also, we should think twice about sending a child to her room. Not only will that usually be more of a removal distance than necessary, but it may tag negative feelings to the child's room. It is preferable to do our best to see that the child's room remains a haven for self-validation.

Rehabilitation is the most usual reason we hear for punishing a child. As shown above, however, the child is in no frame of mind to learn any lessons about life in general, except that it is bad. The only lesson the child might learn is that the particular behavior which brought on the punishment is not acceptable to those around him. But if we consider the principle of abstraction, we can see that the child may be stuck at the abstract message that life is bad and that he is worthless. If the child is unlikely to grasp a general lesson that things don't go well if you do bad things, he is also unlikely to learn the precise lesson that the particular behavior is unacceptable. The only real rehabilitation would come from exposure to relatively consistent validating experiences. Punishment does not offer this.

In fact, the theory of rehabilitation as a goal of adult punishment is also coming under severe doubt today. Unless the person being punished is particularly strong and has the motivation to view her punishment as an opportunity to better herself, she will end the punishment with even worse self-esteem and antisocial behavior than before she was punished. Although our institutions are not yet set up for any other approach, most experts consider punishment the least effective approach to rehabilitate a wrong-doer.

There is a fourth purpose of punishment that is unjustifiable in the adult world but somehow curiously persists in the minds of many parents and teachers—the reminder purpose. This is the idea that pain attached to a lesson will make it more memorable. It is true that the child will be more likely to remember the lesson. But more powerful than the precise lesson we intended to teach will be the more abstract lessons of our mistrust of his learning abilities, our willingness to hurt him for ulterior motives, and his own guilt at not learning free of pain.

In addition, attaching pain to a lesson tends to reduce our credibility. Our child sees us as irrational and out of control. The lesson appears arbitrary, without a rational basis. Otherwise, why could we not convince him of its merit without punishment?

Fortunately, our homes are set up for another approach. Parents are uniquely positioned to help their children change undesirable behavior in the most effective way. The alternative to punishment is rededication to creating frequent validating interactions, together with careful guidance and referencing of the child through his reactions to the immediate misdeed. Children almost always know when they have done wrong. If they don't, punishment makes no sense. And if they do, they need help restructuring their thinking.

Parents can help the child focus on any mistake or misdeed at its most appropriate level of abstraction. By validating the child, the parent can help him avoid viewing a mistake as a threat to his personal integrity and spiritual goodness. Rather than feel rejection at that most abstract level, the child can quickly accept the mistake as a wrong choice between precise alternatives. The child can then decide, with the parent's help, how to increase his likelihood of avoiding that kind of mistake the next time. The parent can guide the child in understanding whether he acted on insufficient information, on misinformation, or on a mistaken interpretation of either information or feelings. If we remember how receptive children are, we will seldom see the need for punishment.

Another important aspect of receptivity is its relationship to its opposite—resistance to genuine communication. Parents can feel great pain when their children seem unreceptive to them. This situation requires tremendous patience. Actually, the child is still extremely receptive to the parent. Only the child is receptive to the messages as the child perceives them, rather than as we intend them. If the child has had a sufficient number of negative experiences, everything we say will be interpreted in the most negative way, in order to validate the child's new negative view of the world. The parent needs great patience to help the child to reconstruct a positive view. The parent must begin with small positive messages which the child cannot misinterpret.

Even a compliment to the child's shoes may get a sly response like, "What was wrong with the ones I was wearing yesterday? You don't like them?" But if we persist in giving "strokes" of affection, the child will eventually tire of constructing negative interpretations for positive messages and will begin to let her positive world-view return. Gradually we can rebuild our relationship of mutual trust, through the cumulative positive messages and validating experiences which we parents can help to create.

A very common situation in which we need to remind

ourselves of the receptivity of our children is when their activities interfere unreasonably with ours or others' or endanger the children themselves and we must say "no" to them. Often we assume that they will not understand why we need to restrain them. Instead of trying to give our reasons, then, we call upon filial obedience as the solution. We might say, "You stop doing it because I said so." But we seldom feel good about saying this. We can sense the switching of gears from caring about the child's wants and needs to seeing some lesson the child can learn from having those wants denied. When we call upon obedience, we may be merely consoling ourselves that saying no is good for the child; after all, "it builds character."

In fact, the kind of filial obedience we parents really want comes only out of mutual trust. This we foster day by day by sharing our thinking with our children, so that they can trust that our reasons are generally good and we can trust that they will sense when they must rely on our judgment.

To illustrate, suppose the children are cutting little pieces of paper into smaller and smaller bits just when we know that our schedule will not permit us to clean up for another two days. This is a time for what we can call the explain-and-divert strategy. We will say no and the children will know it. But we will try to say it

in a nice way,
with a thoughtful explanation of why not,
with an inquiry about how the child might feel,
with a suggestion about what he might do instead, and
with an offer to help him get started.

We might say, "You look like you are having a lot of fun, cutting up all those tiny pieces of paper. You are handling the scissors so well! But you sure are making a mess! All those tiny pieces stick to the carpet and will be too hard for you to pick up. I'm not going to have a chance to clean up until two days from now because I am so busy this week. Maybe you could cut out circles and paste them on a bigger piece of paper. I'll help you find the paste."

In my experience, this approach is more effective than all the yelling and scolding in the world, and a lot more pleasant for parent and child alike. It takes a bit more time in the short run. But in the long run, we save a great deal of time, energy, and pain. At the least the child is spared invalidating messages. But if we proceed with yelling and scolding, we may also find that an older sibling will practice the identical behavior on his younger sibling a few minutes or an hour or two later. Then, our previous haste produces waste: We must spend more time and trouble revalidating two children than we would have spent relating to the one. When we see our behaviors mirrored in sibling disagreements, we often cannot tell whether the child is still feeling frustration from the prior incident or whether she is just imitating us in general. But it really doesn't matter which it is. We should recognize it as an invitation to reflect and to prepare ourselves for the next time, when we can take the stitch in time that will save nine.

Many of us have seen the situation comedies or heard stories in which the well-meaning parent tries to relate to his child by explaining and empathizing, and the impatient child quips that he would rather be spanked or scolded and get it over with. But this does not mean that the child is not receptive to this kind of approach. It may mean that the child is somewhat embarrassed by it, because the parent is demonstrating real caring, when the child has acted flip and uncaring, perhaps even deliberately. Sometimes the child knows well that he was merely acting, and is a bit embarrassed that the parent does not recognize the behavior as a performance. In that case, the parent needs to take cues from the child, say what he feels about the situation, and then let it go. Children feel guilt and embarrassment if they inadvertently leave their parents in pain.

In any case, this kind of validating communication is most effective if we start it early. Once our children have imitated our impatience and noncommunication long enough to make it their own, correcting past deficiencies can be difficult. But it is not impossible. The child remains receptive. And the rewards are great.

O. P. 12

Imitation

The child imitates those
around him or her

THIS last operating principle describes a basic, unavoidable behavior of all children: They tend to imitate those around them, whether we want them to or not. In the modern world, imitation causes many complications, because the mobility of cars and the mass exposure through public media present far more numerous potential behavioral models to children than in any prior age. But it is important for us to accept that the child's tendency to imitate is inevitable before we can develop our best approach as parents to the challenges it creates.

Today's research has demonstrated what many parents have known by intuition: A willingness to imitate is one of the first distinct behaviors that we notice in a child. Usually we first notice imitation when we see a baby imitating the facial expression of an admiring parent or relative. Often we view this early imitation as merely cute and a bit of evidence that the poor child has no behavioral experience of her own yet on which to base independent actions and expressions. In fact, this early imitation is a powerful tool to help the child adapt promptly to the behaviors which her culture expects of her and which will help her take advantage of the availability of parents to meet her needs.

Some of the greatest parental frustrations have been summed up in the words: "Do as I say, not as I do." We desire the child to take our advice, rather than to imitate us. Because a child grasps the essential truth in any situation, the child will be struck by what she perceives as a double standard. The child may express hurt, anger, or, at an older age, disgust, inattention, and alienation. We may hear cries of unfairness, inconsistency, or hypocrisy.

To prevent this kind of frustration and the damage it can do to our relationship with our child, we need to develop ways of preventing unwanted imitation. We must first of all be aware as much as possible whether a child is observing what we are doing. If he is watching and we do not want him to imitate us, then we must promptly make clear why we can do it and he must not. The most difficult situations are three: when the only difference is that we allow ourselves to make mistakes but try to hide them or justify and excuse them to our children, while we demand perfection of our children; when the only difference is age, such as with the "adult" vices like smoking, drinking, swearing, speaking obscenities, or even staying up late; and when there is no real difference, but only a preference on our part. We should look at these three situations in turn.

If we do not allow our children mistakes occasionally, there is no solution to the negativity of the messages we will give. If we demand perfection from our child, we build in frustration for her, because she can never live up to our demands. "Let me make my own mistakes!" says the child. Allowing the child to make mistakes, so long as they are not fatal or permanently damaging, is a strong validation. We give a positive message that we trust the judgment of the child and her ability to learn from her mistakes.

Few of us really expect perfection when we think about it, but we must be careful that our behavior does not give the impression that we do. The child who seeks to fill expectations of perfection will always feel insecure no matter how superb her behavior. If she is aware that we make mistakes ourselves, she will be hurt by the double standard. If we make excuses for our mistakes, try to explain them away, try to justify them with less than candid histories, or try to blame them on somebody else's actions, we should not be surprised if our children start to do the same.

For example, suppose we often forget to put out the dog. Then one day we ask Dick to do it. He may forget, consciously or unconsciously imitating our attitude toward that particular chore. If we will not forgive him easily, the child may well remember that we are easy on ourselves when we forget to do the same thing. He may feel unfairly treated as a result. He may also remember that we justify our mistake by saying that we have so much on our minds or even by blaming the child for distracting us. The child will tend, then, by way of imitating us again, to avoid acknowledging the mistake or forgiving himself, and to make excuses and even try to blame someone else. "I forgot to put the dog out because Mommy called me just when I was about to do it." Seeking scapegoats and being put on the defensive about mistakes makes the child unlikely to focus his attention on avoiding the mistake next time. He will feel confused and in-validated.

If our children imitate something we do which we nevertheless consider a mistake, then, instead of demanding perfection, we must give them room to accept that mistakes are part of life and that each of us is inevitably a unique expression of the perfection of the whole of which each of us is a part. We can forgive our mistakes and do our best to learn from them. They are opportunities to better ourselves.

The second situation where imitation is especially troublesome is when we base a distinction between what we do or have and what we allow the child to do or have on the difference in our ages. "You're just not old enough." We may at first be comfortable with saying that children can't do some things that adults can and leaving it at that. But we must consider what impression this leaves with the child. For instance, in the case of drinking alcohol, do we mean for the child to look forward to drinking as one of the privileges or even purposes of adulthood?

Or with swearing, do we mean to imply that when our child wants to act grown up she should swear more often?

These messages are seldom the ones we want to communicate. But the child hears them nevertheless. It is better that we take the time to explain some real difference between children and adults on which to base the differences in behavior.

Sometimes we try to distinguish between children and adults by saying, "Oh, I'm too old to change my ways, but you are young and can avoid a nasty habit." Sometimes this will work for a time, but it is not satisfactory in the long run. Again the desire to imitate may be too strong. In addition, the more abstract message we communicate is that one become rigid with age, that one cannot learn much or change oneself after one reaches adulthood. Most of us would rather our children did not feel that way, even if we do ourselves.

If we take time to consider, we may find differences between adults and children that a child can relate to without getting the wrong abstract messages about what adulthood holds in store. In the case of alcohol, the actual size of the child is a factor. The fact that she is still growing and needs the best nutrition possible is another factor. These reasons the child may well accept as reasonable.

With swearing, it is harder to find a distinction. Though we are culturally trained to take offense at young children swearing, there seems very little reason why it is bad for children but all right for adults. Rather than use the situation to communicate unwanted abstract messages to our children, tolerance of an occasional swear word may be preferable. Often it is the contrast between the accepted behaviors for adults and children with no apparent reason that causes children to be fascinated by swear words in the first place. We may hear far fewer of them if we tolerate them.

Where we are dealing with a behavior which we can neither tolerate in our children nor explain with a rational distinction, we have the third situation mentioned above. There is no real difference on which to base our desire that the child not imitate us, but we know we don't want him to. If we don't want our children to do it and there is no reason why we can do it if they can't, then we must be dealing with a behavior which we would rather not do ourselves but which we have not stopped.

In this situation, we need to consider shifting levels of abstraction. Rather than focusing our discussion on whether or not the parent or the child should indulge in some behavior, we could focus on what to do about a habit we would rather not have. We have an opportunity to show the child that we have the strength to accept our failings and to work on them.

We can communicate something like this: "I know you would like very much to do what I do. That makes me proud. But this behavior is a problem I haven't come to grips with yet. I would much prefer it if instead of imitating this habit of mine, you would imitate my problem-solving skills in trying to get rid of it." Of course the child will then wait to see some evidence of our problem-solving skills!

We can also model for our children our willingness to seek help to overcome weaknesses. In recent years we have come to realize that problems affecting a family require family solutions. Even such a serious problem as alcohol addiction need not give us fear that the child will imitate destructive behavior if we model and share constructive efforts to change.

If we do not want to change, it is inevitable that the child will have some continuing frustration. Persistent inconsistency between what a parent says and does is one of the most powerful sources of confusion and a sense of helplessness in a child. "How can she expect me to stop biting my nails if she won't stop smoking? Smoking is worse for you than nail-biting, and I'm only a kid!"

But, as always, if the inconsistencies are outweighed by consistent, validating interaction in other contexts and on other subjects, the child will suffer little negative impact.

A variant on the third situation is one where we want to have the child stop imitating us, but when we try to think of reasons we have none, and we realize that we don't really feel strongly about them doing it after all. Such a situation might arise, for example, when we run to the garage without a coat but insist that the child put one on. In that case, we can tell the child our feelings, candidly. "I don't know why I told you you couldn't do that. I think I am trying to be especially careful about your health because I want so much for you to stay healthy. But there really isn't any harm in it as long as you let me know if you get cold." The child will most likely be lifted out of the denial situation and begin observing your way of handling your premature response.

The principle of imitation, then, helps us overcome the occasional but inevitable appearance of having a double standard for ourselves and our children. Even these situations can produce a validating experience, if we help the child see the level on which we want most to be imitated.

As with the other principles, the principle of imitation has two roles. It can lead us out of otherwise seemingly hopeless impasses, as we have just seen. It can also point the way to new possibilities. We can use the desire to imitate as a purely positive force. We can use the power of example to guide our children's behavior. We need not feel inadequate if we do not have the time or ability to put everything we want our children to know into words. If we live as we want them to live, or even just let them see us trying, chances are very good that they will imitate us and follow our example, without a word from us. Like all great teachers, parents teach primarily by example. Part II of this book will describe numerous opportunities for using parental example as a powerful tool for guiding our children toward confidence, competence, and joy.

Here we should consider how parents might handle the influence of others on our children. Two situations seem to give us the most trouble. One occurs when we are aware that someone is "setting a bad example" for our child. The other occurs when we notice some unusual behavior whose original source we do not know. Our less than constructive reactions in both cases arise from a sense of fear. In the first situation, we feel that we are losing control of the models for our children and fear that our children will be led astray. In the second, we wonder if the child has made up the dreadful behavior for some unknown reason, whether we have failed somehow, and if here, too, we have lost some of our influence or control.

If we remember the principle of imitation, we can keep our

faith in our children and in our parenting in both situations. When we recognize how powerful the desire to imitate is, we need not be surprised when our child tries out some new behavior by a new person in his life. It is a sign of growing maturity when a child is able to go through imitation in his mind, without acting it out to determine the consequences. But none of us has entirely eliminated that initial identification with any new role model, and the resulting imaginary substitution. We must expect a young child to try on new behaviors occasionally. If they are undesirable they will pass, if we do not infuse them with special secondary meanings.

Just like our own behaviors which we would rather the child did not imitate, this new outside behavior can be discouraged by the familiar techniques. By showing our appreciation of the new influence in the child's life, we help validate the child. Then by being candid about our concerns, we show our trust in her, that she will give our thinking its proper weight and will take a second look at the new role model. Finally, we can see that we are available often enough to offer a strong model in the direction we desire.

In contrast, if we forbid the behavior or forbid association with the outsider, we will be communicating distrust. The child may well rebel. She may well continue the behavior because it has taken on more importance on the abstract level than it deserves. It has become a symbol of self-assertiveness.

Similarly, when we discover an odd behavior for which we have never set an example, we should avoid imagining that our child has lost his senses. And we should avoid telling him that he has done so. Instead, we need to remember that there is most likely an outside source for some new behavior, and that if we do not let it take on more abstract meaning than it deserves, the child will eventually reject it, if for no other reason than that our life-long example is ultimately a stronger force than the new example.

It is a common observation among parents of grown children that whatever rebellion a child may go through at different stages of his growth, if the child is treated as frequently as possible with love and trust, he will usually adopt the behavior patterns of his family. This is consistent with the frequent observations of school teachers and education specialists that the influences at home are by far the strongest on the child, even if the child spends very little time at home.

The imitation principle, then, gives us valuable reassurance that the example that parents set has permanent impact. It teaches us that how we respond to evidence of outside influence can have significant impact on a child's self-esteem as well as on the parent-child relationship. It tells us that as far as our child is concerned, our acts speak louder than our words. At the same time, when the urge to imitate a new influence is very strong, it helps us muster all our strength to make sure that we do not lose faith in our child or in the years of careful parenting that we have shared so far.

PART
II

The Child's Life Activities

The beginning of love is to let those we love
be perfectly themselves, and not to twist them
to fit our own image. Otherwise we love only
the reflection of ourselves we find in them.
— *Thomas Merton*

CHAPTER 1

Sleeping

OBVIOUSLY sleeping is the least active of a child's activities and perhaps the least complex, so we can take a look at it first. Also, sleeping actually starts each day and can have a lot to do with the way the rest of the day goes.

Children love sleep. They love the routine to prepare for it and the routine to withdraw from it. The routine will change from time to time, but there almost always is one. These observations are well-known. But what if a child hates sleep, fears it, or gets tangled up in a routine that does not relax her before sleep or does not arouse her cheerfully after sleep? And if all appears fine, should we still be communicating anything about sleep as parents? Or rather, is what we are communicating, consciously or not, what we really want to communicate about sleep?

The substance of sleeping can vary a great deal. Around the world, habits differ. Where a child sleeps, with whom, when, how long, or wearing what can vary tremendously. Should we do what our parents did? What our spouse's parents did? What our neighbor does? What they do on television? What the doctor says to do?

We can start to answer these questions with a look at the operating principles.

Sleeping is a reflex designed to rejuvenate the body, mind, and spirit after a certain amount of activity and observation. Because children tend to be so active, they are usually ready for a good sleep at the end of the day. A child tends to like sleep because he, as a spiritual being, recognizes its essential value. He may also have learned from experience that it is a time of strong validation, of family closeness and security, when the day is put into perspective and familial love and trust are reinforced.

The patterns we choose to establish for sleeping must respect these essential needs and perceptions of the child. The child will want to imitate our patterns. It is helpful, then, if he sees our patterns, at least occasionally, such as a weekend nap together, or camping out in one room at a friend's house on a trip.

Likewise, the child wants to please us. If we present a suggestion in a pleasant way, the child will follow it if at all possible—that is, so long as it does not confuse or compromise the child's world-view.

Often we unconsciously communicate expectations that conflict with the suggestions we make. If we let the child know that we really expect her to want to stay up late, for example, or that she will be cranky, that she will fear the dark, or that we will withhold validation if the child does not do what we say, bedtime will be a painful time for all.

Similarly, if we refuse to allow bedtime, but instead try to force it, it may well be that the actual bedtime turns out to be later under force than it would have been under mere allowance. Certainly it will be more of a hassle. Ironically, it is often on the nights when we most want to be sure to get the children to bed on time that we start using force instead of trusting allowance. We may feel resentful that the child "chose" that night to be uncooperative, when really we changed our behavior and made bedtime less of a joyful occasion.

If the child gets hung up in a routine that is not serving the essential purpose of sleeping, we should try referencing the situation to a higher level of abstraction. Probably the routine is not serving its original validating purpose. If the teddy bear's covers just will not lie right, we might explain that the bear knows that we love it just like little Michael knows that we love him and that we can try to get the covers done better tomorrow.

It is amazing how often it is effective to put off the precise problem until tomorrow while emphasizing the abstract love message today. It is important, though, that we remember the thing the following night. If we fear to bring up the subject, hoping the child will have forgotten, we can never know whether she really forgot or not. We are setting ourselves up for guilt feelings and also for the possibility that the child does remember and will take our forgetting as a sign of non-love. If we carry out our expressed intention without fear of a repeat of the tensions of the night before, we will soon discover that the old problem is no longer a problem. The child disposes of it quickly and enjoyably. She is validated both because she remembers the happy solution of last night and because we cared enough to remember. "Let's get the bear tucked in well tonight." "OK!" Success comes right away.

If the child has had a good deal of validation through the day, he will not need much reassurance before bed. On the other hand, if it has been a hectic day, with few moments of focused attention on the child, validation may mean reading a book, answering a series of twenty "Why's," or saying "Goodnight, I love you," three different times. It may also mean a glass of water, going to the bathroom again, or leaving the light on. None of these activities need make us fear that a dangerous new pattern is being established or that fear of the dark has set in.

Rather, we can trust that the child's needs, if filled, will disappear. We can recognize that a sudden request may have value beyond its precise meaning. The child may well want us to do something which has no other reason but that she requested it. This is a way of confirming our love. We can let go of our fears and fill the request without complaint, making sure that we give the abstract messages which are the real purpose of the child's demands.

Awaking is similarly important. The child may want us right there while he stretches for five or ten minutes. Or he may want us specifically not to look at him until he says so. Other times, he will jump out of bed and run around the house before we know he is awake. Each stage represents developments in the self-validation system of our little spirit, and we must trust that he knows his needs.

The newborn baby seeks immediate validation from all the universe, expressed by her mother's touch and embrace. The three- or four-year-old may like to get her self-validation process going before she even considers what others are doing. Or perhaps, she is merely experimenting (that is, setting up a planned observation) to see what we will do if she does not want to be looked at. Whatever her motivations, it is not our role to second-guess the child. If we growl and deny her the choice not to interact, we are withholding validation. We are limiting the child's ability to express herself by her social behavior.

If we say "Fine, see you later," we may validate her choice on the level of tolerance, but we will not have validated her at the level of love. We need to let the child know that we would like to see her, even though we are content to wait until she is ready. We could do this by laughing, and then letting her be. We have let her know that we know she knows she is being silly and inconsistent with our usual pattern, but that we will tolerate it for her sake.

Whether to nap or not to nap depends on the child's needs. Transitions from one pattern to another can be difficult, but listening carefully to the child will help the child reach a new equilibrium with the least hassle for us all. Drowsiness and disorientation after a nap are also common. They, too, must be handled with patience and with trust that if we offer validating messages, they will eventually be accepted and the troublesome time will come to an end.

Irregular sleeping patterns are a warning that something is awry. But irregular means unpleasant for the child, not merely inconvenient for us. Sleep is essentially pleasurable, and if it seems to be giving pain or not resting the child, we must seek a reason. But periodic waking for babies is normal. On their most natural pattern of early life, they would be seeking a meal at the breast every three or four hours through the night. We need only meet their needs, and sleep will satisfy them. Similarly, a baby who gets up and plays from 1 to 3 A.M. merely seeks a little more activity or validation from us. We need not fear that he will be a night person the rest of his life (unless we adopt that expectation, in which case the child will tend to fit the mold we have prepared by following subtle cues from us).

It is only if the child has long periods of tearful wakefulness, crying out, or nightmares, that we need to seek a negative influence. If the child is unhappy in sleep, we need to check that waking experiences have been validating. We should ask ourselves if the child's observations have been well interpreted, if transgressions have been clearly forgiven, if new situations have been adequately explained, and if the child's love has been accepted and reflected back. If not, we can try to talk about any unusual events, play a little game, to help validate the child through focused attention and laughter, or carry the child to validate at the most basic level, through touching and natural rhythm.

Of course at the same time, we need to check for too many bedclothes, too tight bedclothes, too much sleep, too little sleep, hunger, fullness from dinner, wet diaper, or imbalanced diet.

It is especially important for new mothers to recognize the extreme receptivity of the baby to the mother's messages. Mothers can perform magic with a restless, upset, unconsolable child merely by getting their own self-validating system into operation. When she hands the baby to the father and the child calms down, it may not be because the father is magic, which would make the mother feel even more inadequate. Rather, the child has been removed from the environment of tension and frustration surrounding the mother. Often if the father plays a bit with the child and returns the baby to the mother once she has collected herself, the tension for both will be gone. She can stop pitying herself, stop seeking to blame herself for failing to meet the baby's every mood, stop fearing a sleepless night, and stop making excuses to her husband about how hard she has tried. She can stop trying so hard and allow things to move along rather than forcing them. She can say to herself, "Relax, all he needs is me, his mother, and the world will not come apart if I just sit with him a while." Ninety-nine times out of a hundred that while is very very short, because a contented sleepy baby, back in tune with mother who is back in tune with herself, has fallen fast asleep.

At the start of this chapter, we dismissed the variations in sleep habits rather easily, in order to emphasize the importance of letting the child set her own pattern. It may be worthwhile here, however, to help remove a common obstacle which can interfere with our general determination to trust our child to know her sleeping needs. This obstacle is the various fears which we may assoicate with having a baby or young child in bed with us.

Often relatives suggest that we should fear rolling over on a baby. Thorough studies have shown that the chances of any bad consequences are virtually nil. If we roll onto just a shoulder or a hand, the child will let us know right away by grunting or wiggling around. Those of us who have been in bed with our children usually have the opposite concern—we are so tuned in to our children that we awaken when they move at all. This supersensitivity will adjust like many other inborn responses, if we give it time. Separating mother and child is unlikely to solve the problem, because the mother's sensitivity is compounded by her concern that she may not hear when the child "really" needs her. We must trust that the mother and child will adjust to each other for the good of both.

The fear of rolling over on the baby appears to be a holdover from medieval times, when this was the common explanation given by the very poor for the disappearance of unwanted children, who were usually given to "foundling" homes. While abandonment could be tried in court, accidental death by rolling over was a matter for the church. As an abhorrent method of limiting family size, this history makes us shudder. But we can take comfort in the fact that rolling-over deaths are unknown in the modern world even among families who share a bed with their newborns and children. If our child wants this pattern, we can be comfortable with it and need not feel guilty that we are taking risks.

Another common fear is that the child will be more emotionally dependent if she has company at night as well as during the day, and that we need to force her to be on her own early.

The operating principles indicate that this fear has no basis. Healthy children seek to go out on their own no matter what we do. Only, they will not do so until they are ready. If forced to do so before that time, they will likely comply to please us, but they will also be likely to harbor resentment because of our lack of trust. They may also lose confidence, because they will assume that they merit the lack of trust. At the very least, they may put off their normal time for contented sleeping by themselves, because they are not sure that once they make the move they will ever be welcome again when they need it.

If the child reverts, seeking to cuddle and sleep with us again when he has been sleeping alone for months, we need not fear that he has truly reverted. Rather, we can realize that the action is merely a call for special validation, whether because of a new sitter, a family argument, a new sibling, or whatever. All stages pass if we allow them to. Even if we cannot identify any significant change in the child's life, we can trust that he has his reasons for the new behavior and try to validate the child.

Not only must we trust our children in their choice of sleeping habits, but we must trust our own intuition and common sense, getting in touch with our own spiritual being, in order to weed out all the extraneous and misleading doubts and fears we may encounter. We must be willing to ask ourselves, for example, whether it was really a good thing when we heard as children, "Now that you're old enough, you have to sleep by yourself." Or, do I really have to watch the late news and then miss my children's first morning smiles and resent them when they wake me?

Putting us back in touch with ourselves is one of the unexpected ways in which conscious parenting makes parenting a real joy. That look of an angel on the face of a sleeping child is not entirely an illusion.

CHAPTER 2

Eating

EATING serves two major functions for children. It provides them with the raw materials with which to build their bodies, and it reinforces social behaviors. We tend to emphasize the first function at the expense of the last. We try hard to see that our children eat well. But we often ignore the social patterns which the child learns from the way the family eats and the way we try to enforce our concept of nutrition. We need to pay as much attention to how they eat and to how we guide their eating choices as we do to what they eat. If we do not, it is unlikely that our children will learn to choose wisely for themselves. In addition, mealtime can become a chronic source of tension and negative feelings in the family. In contrast, we have the power to make it a strong validating experience for our children.

A number of authors have described current knowledge about the nutritional needs of children and how to meet them from the food available in the marketplace. Recent research indicates that inadequate nutrition contributes to a number of childhood problems which we believed not long ago to be a matter of chance or genetics. Some of these problems are low resistance to infections, failure to thrive, ear infections, allergies, learning disabilities, bedwetting, lack of concentration, stuttering, hyperactivity, low or high weight for age, nightmares, moodiness, irritability, food cravings, fits of crying, and even physical aggression.

All these can have other causes, of course, but we should consider basic nutritional support in every case. This chapter will not attempt to describe the particular needs which any of these conditions suggests. It must suffice to say that each child needs his optimal mix of protein-rich foods, carbohydrates (complex, simple, and indigestible fiber), fatty acids, minerals, vitamins and trace minerals (cofactors in energy metabolism, tissue building, and nervous and endocrine control), and water. The diet should be as unprocessed as the family is comfortable with and have as little artificial ingredients and sugar as possible. For the first year and, if the child chooses, much of the second, the best way to meet these needs is by breastfeeding.

Aside from the nutritional needs themselves, the most frequent concern of parents is how to get our children to eat what they are supposed to. The principle of trust plays a key role here. We hear that a child, if left to himself, will choose a healthy diet from a variety of foods. In contrast, we also hear that children are consuming more and more sodas, sugar, artificial dyes, caffeine, salt, and other products which we accept as detrimental to good health. Can we trust our children to choose their foods in their best interest?

Yes, so long as we provide them with accurate information, a good example in ourselves, and a healthy emotional environment in which to make their eating choices. If we want to have a child who chooses healthily for himself when the child leaves our control, we must maintain our trust in him in order that he may internalize that trust for himself. Without that self-trust, he will be at the mercy of all would-be authorities, including television advertising, fad diets, and crazes among his peers.

But is trust in this case worth preserving, since experience shows that children are drawn to the sweet and salty, the fatty, and colored choices for food? The answer is again in the affirmative. Telling the child to obey her doctor, the right books, or her parents in the question of eating choices for the rest of her life is futile. The food manufacturers have far more frequent and more persuasive means than these to influence the eating choices of our children. Instead, we must maintain our trust in the child and communicate it to her by praising wise choices, by giving her any information which will be helpful in making wise choices, and by avoiding negative messages at mealtime which can turn eating into a clash of wills.

But can we be genuine in our trust if we know that children don't eat right without strong guidance from us? We need some information base ourselves to understand why the child's inclinations seem unreliable here. We must take a quick look at human history for that.

If food selection is based on instinct—that is, on genetic inheritance—we must consider that those instincts that we have will be geared to operate on a virtually unrefined, unprocessed diet, since we have developed advanced mechanical and chemical food processing so recently in our history. This means our children's instincts would presumably be fairly reliable on a natural diet which included no refined sugar, very few pressed oils, no refined flours, and very few foods out of their growing season except those that can be dried simply. But by the same token, their natural inclinations may be unreliable when faced with foods like sodas, fried salty chips, and artificially flavored candies, which are very recent inventions.

It is up to us parents, then, to transmit cultural cues to our children which will guide them toward healthful eating habits. Luckily reliance on cultural patterns is nothing new to the human baby. When we look around the world, we see that different peoples and their children survive well on an incredible diversity of food mixes. However, the healthiest groups are those which have so far avoided the most recent food processing advances and have instead relied on their centuries-old cultural heritage. Different cultures worldwide put great store by their eating traditions. We can guess that this is because the traditional way of making use of the foodstuffs which were available in the environment of each particular culture was an important thing to teach to each new generation of children. It served not only to instruct them how to be healthy but also to teach them to respect the social aspects of food.

If healthful eating is as much a cultural or learned behavior as an instinctual one, we have a firmer basis for feeling trustful toward our child. We can have confidence that our child will make healthful choices by providing him with strong cultural cues which send him toward healthful food. For example, telling Tim that he must not eat sweets because we say so will leave the child feeling insecure. He is unlikely to respond calmly to the precise message we intend to convey.

Instead we might say: "Sweets taste very good to us. But they are only a small part of the original food. Sugar is the tasty part of the food removed from the other nourishing parts of the food. When we would find these foods wild, they would taste good and be good for us. But when we eat only the sugar, it makes your body not work as well. It changes how your brain works, how your blood works, how your skin works, and how strong your teeth are. It is a modern invention to give us one simple taste which tastes good but which is supposed to go along with all kinds of other good things in our foods which we can't taste. We hear about it all the time because it makes a lot of money for some people. It does not get old, and it is hard to stop eating it. So it is easy to sell a lot or to keep until it is all sold. But we must exercise care not to eat too much of it."

Most children who are old enough to understand the vocabulary are fascinated by this kind of explanation and do their best to implement it right away. We should expect this, because of the principle of receptivity. If we take the time to let them know that the healthy eating choices have real significance, they will respond in a way which inspires our trust.

We must be careful, too, to set an example to our children of how to respond to others who offer sweets with good intentions. We must not be afraid to say no to the grandparents, to the bank, or to anyone else who offers our children sweets. We need not apologize or go into a lesson on nutrition. We need only assert our personal choice: "Thank you very much. But we don't eat candy except on holidays."

One of the most common imbroglios about eating involves

dessert. We urge our children not to overindulge in dessert. We may explain the hazards of too much ice cream or sugar or calories. Yet we tease the children about their supposed inability to resist the stuff. And we serve them the sweets at times when it is clear that we most want to please them—at birthdays, for example. Finally, we serve dessert virtually every time the entire family joins together for a meal.

The child cannot help but develop very positive associations with desserts, despite all the nasty things they are supposed to do to us. Many people's most validating recollections of their childhoods revolve around holiday meals, when the parents were kidding the children about their insatiable appetites for desserts. Is it any wonder that we are so easily persuaded to treat ourselves with a little packaged cake when we feel down? If we want our children to avoid this pattern, we must address the problem at its most abstract. We must remove desserts from their undeserved role as misguided expressions of validation and love.

Here are some suggestions for preventing these destructive patterns. First, we can avoid saying: "You can't have any dessert unless you finish your meal," or any of the dozens of variations on that theme. The messages from these statements are numerous and all undesirable: Desserts are something to be sought; a healthy meal is just a way to earn dessert; my parents use something they know is bad as a reward for me; something which is bad may not be bad if you have earned it; dessert is a reward for being good; and, perhaps worst of all messages, my parents think my good behavior can be, should be, or has to be bought.

Secondly, we can avoid serving sweets that the family did not make at home. The only legitimate specialness which can attach to sweets is that they represent so much labor on the part of the provider for the household that it must have been a labor of love.

Finally, we can give validating messages directly, not indirectly through desserts. We can say how nice it is to be all together or how much fun it is to be served all from the same bowl or how we wish we could all eat together more often or how filled with love or good feelings the room is when everyone relaxes to eat. We need not wait until dessert for giving validating messages, when even if those messages get through, it will be in conflict with the nutritional concerns we have been trying to convey at so many other meals.

These steps will go a long way toward removing or preventing our children from eating sweets to salve emotional hurts. Instead, it will help them recognize desserts at their appropriate level of abstraction, as pleasant luxuries to enjoy occasionally.

As parents, we need to remember that eating, like all other activities, is a process. We should focus not only on the food that the children eat, but on how they eat it. Otherwise, even if we have accustomed them to a certain mix of healthy foods, they will be unable to make healthful choices when they go out into a world that does not offer that particular mix and that can play tricks with their appetites. In addition to nutrition lessons, we can try to convey these lessons: Eat only when hungry; drink only when thirsty; if the food is significantly refined or processed, don't rely on your appetite to tell you when to stop; eat only when relaxed; chew thoroughly; and stop before you feel stuffed. We might also want to encourage our children to avoid self-righteousness about their eating habits, since a particular meal is only a precise activity, while making your friends uncomfortable by implied criticism of their way of eating is a dangerous abstraction.

Some of the greatest frustrations with children's eating habits seem to come from a difference between what we parents say and what the children observe us doing. Obviously the cultural significance of good eating does not appear as strong as it might if we parents do not observe what we are trying to present as a cultural tradition. For example, if I set high store by not eating between meals, but I have a quick snack when I come home from a meeting, or the father asks what he can nibble before dinner, the child will face a conflict between our words and our actions. According to the principle of spirituality, the child will sense the essence of the matter. Either we parents are weak and cannot act according to our own ideas of what will fill our needs, or we have a double standard for children and adults, which we have failed to explain.

If the child has not received sufficient other validation, this conflict will be painful for the child. If the child's experiences are such that the tension over eating is the last straw, we will be faced with rebellion at the table. Often this takes the form of deliberate disregard for even common sense table manners. If we fail to recognize that the child needs referencing or validation and instead feel challenged by the rebellion, we may see one of the most common and painful of family battles. Not only does the child receive reinforcement for an emerging negative worldview, but the parent tends to lose faith in the child. And, on a more precise but nevertheless very important level, the conflict makes it virtually impossible for any of the participants to adequately digest and make use of the food they have eaten. Digestion slows when adrenalin flows. By the time the child or parent is again relaxed, chemical changes in the food make it less biologically useful, and natural organisms that inhabit the lower digestive tract will get the benefit of the undigested food, producing gas, discomfort, and most unfortunately, further irritability.

It is important to remember then that, above all, eating should be a relaxed positive experience. A child who feels good about himself will want to take care of himself. This kind of motivation will be more important in the long run than any number of lectures which ride on an undercurrent of distrust and worry.

CHAPTER 3

Bathing and Cleaning

WHEN our babies are first born, they seem very delicate. We want to keep them free of dirt and harmful germs, without even thinking about it. In addition, public media and current cultural standards emphasize spotless, white, germ-free environments and sweatless, odorless, oil-free bodies as the ideal. Coming from the germ-free environment of the mother, the new baby seems all the more vulnerable than the rest of us to the bad effects of not being clean. This chapter will address some of the situations in which hygiene becomes a parenting issue.

The responsibility to keep a new baby clean can seem overwhelming. We often think clean actually means antiseptic or germ-free. Actually, none of us is germ-free for a moment as long as we are living in a normal environment. The baby picks up his family germs immediately from his mother. These are not bad. Something must populate his skin, and it might as well be nonthreatening germs from the mother as some unusual germs that can sneak in from the hospital after an antiseptic wash or that can come from other sources if we repeatedly remove the set of germs the baby adopts from his immediate family.

Louis Pasteur's discovery that diseases can be caused by microscopic organisms should not leave us fearful of all microscopic organisms. Once we try to imagine Nature's ideal plan for a new baby, we find that babies come equipped to deal with the germs of a healthy family. We can assume an attitude of trust in our instincts and in our baby. We need not feel guilty about the fact that it is impossible to keep the baby from getting wet from diapers. We also can avoid feeling that a thorough bath today is a matter of life and death. Once we are free from this kind of guilt, we can respond to our child's real needs and avoid creating negative experiences which may actually sabotage our efforts to teach our child habits of good hygiene.

For example, modern medical experts say that the substances found on the baby's skin at birth may be protective. They may help the skin to make a more gradual transition from exposure only to amniotic fluid to exposure to the air. So we don't need to bathe the child immediately. Sometimes when a nurse whisks the baby away right after birth, we protest that we want her with us a bit more. The nurse then protests: "But we have to wash her off! You want her to be clean, don't you?" It can be very intimidating. But we must trust that between the healthy mother and her baby, the needs of each can be met without conflict, so long as there is not significant interference from the outside. Experts say that the baby doesn't really need a bath for four to six weeks as long as her environment is generally clean, so the fact that we feel uncomfortable and inept at bathing a newborn should not detract from our joy at being new parents.

If we do not feel compelled to place being washed at the top of our priority list for our child, we are free to choose times for baths which are relaxed and fun for everyone involved. If a baby or child is overactive from a busy day, or if we are going out at night and feel we are trying to beat the clock, we can skip the bath without any guilt. With an older child, we need not fear that she will get the wrong idea, if we take the time to explain why it would be better to take a bath tomorrow. "It's been a long day. You are tired and we are in a hurry. It will be more fun tomorrow." The child will be pleased. But then most of us wonder, will the child quickly learn that fussing or acting tired will get the bath put off any time she may want?

Here we can remind ourselves that we can trust the child to like something that is good for her, as long as she generally feels good about herself. Of course if we ourselves have negative associations with washing, so that we are not sure it is a good experience, we need to come to terms with this prejudgment ourselves. But if we accept that she will enjoy a bath if it is offered at the right time in a positive way, we need only see to it that we do not create negative associations with bathing which will overshadow the child's recognition of its essential usefulness.

If bathing is normally an enjoyable time, offering the child validating experiences, we need not worry about her learning to manipulate the bath time. If we allow the child to keep herself clean, rather than forcing the behavior, that in itself is a strong validation of the child. In contrast, if we tease in such a way that the child realizes that we expect a five-year-old to hate baths, the child may very well adopt that attitude.

We can expect the child to be receptive to genuine explanations of the choices we make with respect to the child. However, if the child is already in a fit because he does not want a bath and we have been insistent, we may be amazed by an about-face if we decide to be agreeable and suggest skipping it. Now, when we say, "Oh well, I guess we're all too tired to do this now," the child may very well insist that a bath now be had. We may dismiss this as childhood contrariness. But what we are seeing is actually a shift in levels of abstraction. On a precise level, the child did not want a bath. We resisted vehemently, casting momentary doubt on our confidence in the child's decision and in the importance of his wants. This message at the highest level was one of non-love. Yet the child also knows on a precise level that we think a bath is important to his health. If then we "give in" without a positive, validating message, even our giving in will be misinterpreted as non-love. Then the child will change his mind. He would rather take the unwanted bath than think that we think so little of him that we will give up on the bath.

To change our minds then, takes some conscious referencing of the situation. We must end the negative messages and switch to positive. We might say: "Well, I see that you really don't want this bath tonight. I think it is important to wash regularly, but one day off won't matter. It will be more fun tomorrow because we can do it in the daytime (or whatever)." With this conversation, we have validated the child's feelings. We have reconfirmed how we feel but explained why what might have appeared inconsistent or unloving—giving up on the bath—was not so. We have given the child room to view the change in our plans as a positive one: We respect his desires. We have also set an example of cooperation. We have compromised our desires to accommodate his, without compromising our basic beliefs.

How different this is from being afraid to change our minds under pressure from the child because "he shouldn't always get his way"! It is astonishing how the worst situations can be turned around by this kind of approach. And it is worth noting that we need not fear that we look indecisive if we take a moment or two to think the situation through before we give a certain response. The child will most likely appreciate that we take him that seriously.

As with other activities, the child will go through various stages of interest in washing. Baths may be irresistible to the child one month and a drag the next. The change can come overnight, too, for instance, when an admired friend happens to say that she doesn't like baths. We must wait out these stages with a strong dose of trust that the overall messages about washing and cleanliness will eventually prevail. If the child's life experience on the whole has been positive, they undoubtedly will.

In all areas of cleanliness, the parents' example is a powerful tool. It is very helpful if the child is allowed to observe the way we parents take care of ourselves. If we are brushing our teeth, why close the bathroom door, for example? We can consider taking baths with our small child, or letting the child talk to us while we are in the shower. Besides the healthy example we offer this way, we get more time with the child and very likely more showers!

If we think through each aspect of living with a child before we commit ourselves to a particular pattern, we will usually find that many sources of tension can be avoided by not drawing unnecessary lines.

Another common area of frustration with children is in keeping the house clean and neat. Too often mothers feel as if their primary role must be to pick up things others have dropped. As in the cleaning of my body, the cleaning of my room and my living space must ultimately be my responsibility. If we want our child to adopt that idea, there are several things we can do, but often the pressures of the moment find us doing things that may actually teach exactly the wrong lesson. Again timing of the cleaning activity and moments to think before we speak can be crucial for making cleanliness and neatness a validating activity in the child's life, rather than a negative one. If we run around picking up toys from the hall and cleaning up the child's room but complain that we have not been able to care for our own clothes or our own hair, will she not wonder whose responsibility is whose? Rather, we can avoid sounding like a martyr or Cinderella. Instead, we can let her know that we take care of ourselves and our space so that we can be healthy happy people and good parents. We can also let her know that we help her take care of herself because we know she is not completely ready to take care of herself by herself. So many clothes, such a big room, such a big house, or whatever, is a lot for a small person to be responsible for, even if it is only with respect to her own things. We can share these thoughts with our child and will find her amazingly receptive.

Whether we are encouraging our children to wash their hands before dinner, to scrub a carrot before eating it, to wash their apple after they drop it, to wash their faces, or to keep a bandage on a cut, in each case we must try to stay aware of the multiple messages we are communicating and the multiple responses of our children. Keeping our children and our living spaces neat and clean need not be a source of pain for either child or parent. If we keep our priorities clear and avoid vague fears by applying the operating principles, cleanliness will be next to godliness in more ways than one.

CHAPTER 4

Dressing

NUMEROUS questions face a parent when it is time to dress a child. What shall the child wear? Who will put on what? When will the child learn to tie his shoes? What if the child hates mittens? Should girls wear dresses or pants? Should we dress up to go visiting? Should I allow the child to express his own taste no matter how outrageous the result?

Many of us try to do what we think is most sensible with the least fights and try not to worry what other people will think. But we still may have a nagging sense of helplessness or guilt, because we appear to be in control but feel that we really don't know what is going on or what effect what we are doing is going to have on the child.

The operating principles can clear the air. Dressing is an everyday activity. We want most to allow our child to adopt the most effective and comfortable patterns of behavior possible in order for him to achieve a neat, comfortable, pleasant, and adequately protective dress. We don't know how he will ultimately choose to dress himself. All we can do is make the kinds of things we value in dress sources of validation for him.

This parental function is enough to keep us totally occupied. It will release us from guilt about either imposing on the child's taste or, on the other hand, allowing others to think we are an ill-kept family because our child is allowed to dress so oddly. We will be busy trying to share with the child our tastes and preferences while validating any expression of his.

For example, if three-year-old Jennie chooses a plaid jumper to wear with a paisley blouse, we need to think a moment before we respond. If we laugh, we must be sure that we allow her to laugh with us. "That sure is a lot of different designs and colors on one little person," we could say. We should avoid saying, "That looks ridiculous!" The first response accepts the precise choices she made and stays at that level. The second carries with it a more abstract message that she makes poor choices. Only a strongly validated child could excuse that message and share our laugh. Next, we can validate her choice, even though we don't like it. "It must have been fun to pick it out yourself." Then, and only then, can we be effective in suggesting alternatives. "Do you think maybe the shirt and jumper would match better if you chose a plain shirt or a plain jumper?" She may well say yes. We have chosen one value—matching—which she can appreciate, and we have avoided implying that the choice was wrong by all values. We have also communicated that matching is important to us at a time when she can be receptive to the idea, because so far the dressing experience has remained a validating one.

Even if she responds with a no to our suggestion, all is not lost. It may well be that if we let the matter go for a while and create some other validating experience, she will ask later, before we must go out, if she can change her clothes to meet the new value of matching. This kind of hindsight in children is not rare if we give it a chance. A child who resists change when in a negative frame of mind may try to "rewrite history" when she is in a positive frame of mind. She may insist on getting dressed again. Here we must again try to control ourselves. We may feel resentful that she is being so inconsistent. But if we notice that it is merely a replay of what she now sees as a possible mistake of hers, to wipe it out in a sense, we can accept it. In this new light, we can recognize that, in fact, our calm suggestion of a matching outfit did have the desired effect, no matter how awkwardly delayed.

Finally, even if we let the matter go and Jennie does not choose to redo that precise activity today, we can trust that another day matching will come up as a value she will try to apply. We must accept the fact that today she may look silly to others and others may even think poorly of us as parents, but for one day we can take it. We can take it because the interaction that resulted in that outfit was a positive one and will most likely result in dress habits in the future which will please us, our child, and even other people.

CHAPTER 5

Using the Toilet

EARLY toilet training can affect one's personality forever. Today we recognize this idea as one of the most important as well as sensational contributions of Freud. Through the then newly discovered techniques of psychoanalysis, Freud revealed that adult mental disturbances often had their roots in early childhood. When parents had forced their child to control his toilet functions before he felt motivated to do so, he tended to feel rejected, unloved, and inadequate and could develop any number of neuroses to cope with these feelings.

Freud found that even outwardly successful adults were often still troubled by these feelings. They had vague marauding fears and insecurities. He and his followers found that if an adult was given the opportunity, through expertly guided, searching interviews, to recognize the early experiences which gave rise to these feelings, she often could dispel her fears and focus on the precise source of her insecurities. She then could see that her parents spent too much time giving her negative messages, that she rightfully resented her parents then and should feel no guilt about it, that she was a normal child nevertheless, and that her parents did not know any better. Then she could forgive her parents, forgive herself for her guilt, and rebuild her self-esteem.

Toilet training was only one element of the early childhood experience which Freud examined. But it was a crucial one in the Victorian age when he was working, because polite society considered virtually all natural functions except eating totally taboo. A child not trained to the toilet on time would be considered less than a savage.

Unfortunately, vestiges of this approach still remain in our society. We have all heard about the cajoling, pleading, admonitions, and frustrations parents go through. But with all this, the average age for toilet training in this country today is three years old, with normal ranging from two to four or five years old. We might wonder what pain and frustration the child is experiencing if the parents feel so much. There may be no good reason to allow toilet training to be a persistent, daily, negative message to our children over a year or two of those important early years. Can we make toilet training a validating experience? Can we show love while guiding our child into the acceptable behavior patterns of our culture?

According to the operating principles, we can. First, we can trust that Nature has equipped our child with the necessary skills to cope effectively with a more or less simple living pattern, as long as we do our parenting job as Nature intended. The child will seek to imitate our behavior and will probably prefer his body relatively clean. Whether or not a child alone would ever develop regular controlled toilet habits is not a question that should affect our parenting options. We are dealing not with a child alone in the wild, but rather with a child in his normal environment, a social one, with parents close by. Human beings are a social species, and they learn quickly what behavior pleases the group, as long as their basic spiritual identity remains intact.

In the social context, then, we can trust that there will come a time in a child's life when he is aware of his excretory functions and when he will choose to control them in the manner he has observed in the people around him.

Our concern as parents is what we can do to guide the child so that this time comes as soon as is socially desirable without any damage to the child. Presumably, there might be damage if the time came too "late," but studies show that the parents' attitude is far more powerful than that of peers or society in causing the child either to remain confident about herself or to feel inadequate or out of step. If we trust the child's timing and are sensitive to the child's cues about her interests, it is hard to imagine that late training could be bothering the child if she has not yet expressed any interest in it.

Is there any reason to force training, then? Perhaps we need to come to grips with our own expectations and desires. Are we concerned with what others will think—mother, father, mother-in-law, father-in-law, neighbors, friends, nursery school? Do we have vague fears stemming from messages we received as children ourselves, that the child will never be trained? Do we feel that diapers are an altogether messy, dirty business that should be forgotten as quickly as possible?

We need to take some time to determine what our reasons may be. If we find that we are considering forcing a behavior on our child to fill our needs rather than hers, we may want to reconsider. If we apply the principle of abstraction, we may be able to put our concerns into a more comfortable order of priority. I would like to prevent my mother-in-law from thinking I am inadequate as a mother because little Kathy is not yet trained. I would like to be able to travel without a diaper bag. But these may be less important to me than making sure that she continues to receive messages of love and trust. In addition, if she is more sensitive to these messages than to her grandmother's occasional frowns or the hassle of changing diapers while traveling, it may well be that she will conform sooner, more comfortably, and more permanently to our cultural norms than if we try to force the new pattern on her.

Because urinary and bowel functions are such an integral part of the child's physical life, the messages that we communicate in connection with these functions can have important effects on the child's relationship to his body. Though the child may learn to use the toilet under pressure, he may also learn that we do not trust the child's perception of his needs, that there is something wrong with his body, that there is something dirty or bad about his normal functions, or that he cannot trust himself to interpret his needs. Even innocent statements like "Don't you want to be clean?" or "Four-year-olds don't usually wet their pants," can leave unintentional negative traces on a child's mind.

It is exactly these traces which concerned Freud. Today we laugh nervously about another of Freud's discoveries, the oral and anal fixations. The oral character is supposed to give whatever is asked and to be generous generally. The anal character is supposed to keep back what is most valued and to be acquisitive generally. If we consider the operating principles and what they tell us about a child's reaction to the stress of having a behavior forced upon him, we can see that these two extremes of character are alternative defenses to what the child perceives as an attack on his spiritual essence. The child will seek to meet expectations by producing on the command of his parent when put on the toilet. He will also seek to imitate those around him by holding on until he gets to a toilet and by considering the stool or urine something of value when it is finally produced.

Since the child has had the behavior thrust upon him before he perceives the need, it is impossible for him to call upon his own judgment as to what is the appropriate response. Depending upon the parental attitude and the child's inclinations from other experiences, the child will emphasize either giving freely or holding back as a response to stress.

The real value of the operating principles in this situation is to remove the worry about which of these two characters our child will adopt as a result of early stresses, and to rid us of the expectation that he will inherit our own hang-ups. The child need not make a choice at all if he perceives no threat and needs no defense. He can be open and confident to give or retain as most appropriate to the situation, in response to his own needs and the needs of those around him. Our child does not have to develop any life-long emotional defense patterns in the course of learning social control of a natural function.

A major reason why toilet training since Victorian times has been such a focus for parents has been the fact that social conventions have made it difficult for children to learn by imitation. It is worthwhile considering whether our personal sensibilities are so essential to us that we cannot relax them and allow our young children to observe us as we go about our toilet routine. Mothers often feel frustration trying to teach their sons, in particular. Is it any wonder this is difficult if neither the son nor the mother has seen or heard about the father's toilet habits?

The fear that the child will not respect our privacy is a common barrier to open use of example in toilet training. But the principles of trust, imitation, and expectation again are instructive. We can trust that our child will value things we value—in this case privacy. Usually a child will express a desire to be left alone at times, often quite early. We can then expect her to imitate us, so long as we are careful to respect her developing sense of privacy. She will give us time alone just as we allow it to her. Finally, the child will want to please us. If she is eager to tell us some story, but we ask her to wait until we are finished in the bathroom, she will wait contentedly, provided her self-esteem has been validated generally in other ways, and that this postponement is handled with gentleness.

On the other hand, if we insist that we be present when the child is in the bathroom, because she might make a mess or get herself "dirty," and then insist also that she wait outside the door while we use the toilet, her understanding of privacy will be muddled. For her, the difference in treatment will appear to stem from her size, from our lack of confidence in her, from her own inadequacy, from the unimportance or arbitrariness of privacy, or from some secret we parents hide from her in the bathroom. None of these are factors we would consciously concern the child with, but we must take care not to do so unconsciously.

If we take toilet training slowly, without breaking the stride of confidence we have set between ourselves and our young child, the experience can be just as validating and loving as any other.

These abstractions sound hopeful, but we may wonder what happens if three-year-old David wets his clothes at grandmother's house on Sunday afternoon. Usually grandmother will say nothing. Perhaps she will raise an eyebrow. It is usually we parents who sense criticism, disapproval, guilt, or inadequacy when we feel we are being watched, even if the onlookers say nothing. We need not take on these emotions, even if grandmother does intend them. If we take the event in stride, with no wavering of our own self-confidence, grandmother will not have room to heap on the criticism. Even if she does, we need not defend ourselves with a list of our good efforts, our secret frustrations, excuses for our child, or our usual compensatory remarks—"But he is so good otherwise!"

Instead, we need to remember ourselves, and our trust that time will tell. When David is six, and grandmother marvels that he is so cooperative, courteous, happy, and respectful, we can remember to ourselves that the "permissive" toilet training helped. But it is no use saying, "See! I was right." The grandmother would likely never believe that there was any connection. It is likely too that grandmother will have long since forgotten the wetting incident. Grandmothers have lived long enough to have learned more than we tend to think they have. They are often more accepting than we think. And grandmothers, even more than we parents sometimes, want our children to know how to be joyful above all.

CHAPTER 6

Exploring Sex

S EX is such a touchy subject in American society today that it is almost impossible to even guess at an appropriate response to childhood sexuality without first thinking through our own attitudes toward sex and what attitudes we would or would not like to have our children adopt. At one extreme, we can set stern limits on what is acceptable behavior to us and leave the child on her own to satisfy whatever needs she may have for understanding her sexuality. At the other extreme, we can try benign neglect, hoping that the child will figure out for herself what behavior will be acceptable to society.

Many parents are especially concerned with their child's sexual exploration because of the daily headlines about early sex, child abuse, broken relationships, and homosexuality. It appears that their prevalence may mean some active, forceful intervention is needed to prevent these from showing up in our child. But the operating principles help to remind us that instead of worrying and second-guessing our child's innermost thoughts, it is our job to have our parenting skills finely tuned when her sexuality manifests itself, whether in actions that offend us or others, in changes in her other behavior patterns, in gentle questions, or in angry

declarations. Then we must be prepared to avoid excessive curiosity or easy judgment in order to discover how we can best
help. We can listen instead of prying and guide instead of chiding.
The respect we show for the child's privacy will itself go a long
way toward communicating our own respect for sex, even if we
falter in our attempts to articulate our thoughts on sex. And our
listening will demonstrate the sensitivity which we feel is appropriate in sexual matters. We need to find a consistent, happy
medium between respecting the child's individuality and helping
her learn the behaviors most likely to produce constructive relationships with those around her.

The operating principles will help. First, we must trust that
the child has a basic blueprint which will allow him to function
acceptably in society so long as we guide him well. Second,
although we must allow development rather than force it, we
must be mentally prepared to guide him when he seeks guidance.
Third, we must remain constantly aware of the different levels
of abstraction regarding messages to him about sex. Finally, this
area of human behavior is perhaps the most scrambled even
among adults today. Not only must we be ready to meet our
child's need for a reference point to maintain perspective, but
we may often find that we need to stop for a moment and refer
ourselves to the proper level of abstraction.

For example, suppose Josh is pulling at his pants during
dinner. We could say: "Don't play with yourself." What messages
will Josh hear? He is probably responding to some physical sen-
sation. Do we want him to ignore physical sensations? Should
he distrust his physical sensations? Do we think he is unable to
interpret the feelings of his own body accurately? Is play bad? Is
his genital area his "self" rather than just a part of him?

These questions may seem excessively worrisome. Hasn't
that kind of admonition been used for generations? It has, but
there is reason to believe from voluminous work since Freud's
groundbreaking research that it is not as harmless as we tend to
think.

If we come to terms with the most likely misinterpretations
of what we say, we can more easily get ourselves into the habit
of saying more precisely what we mean, with the least room for

misinterpretation. After all, "don't play with yourself" is an abstraction for the convenience of the parent rather than for the child's good. It is a euphemism to help the adult avoid a taboo subject. But the child hears a negative abstract message. Wouldn't it be better to focus our message on the precise behavior we wish to discourage, even at the risk of nearing the border of adult sensibilities?

Any one of the following responses would give less negative messages. "Josh, your wiggling bothers me." "If you need to touch yourself in your more private places, Josh, it's better to do it privately, because it is distracting to people for someone to be touching his genitals." "If your pants are uncomfortable, Josh, maybe you would like to be excused to adjust them or scratch or whatever you want." Any of these may stimulate a question from him, especially if he is not yet used to getting this kind of communication from us. We must be prepared, then, for the "whys."

If we are in an environment where we will be embarrassed by giving a proper explanation, the only solution is to postpone the explanation until later. A delayed explanation is difficult, of course, because we are asking for an immediate change of conduct. If there is a threat to life or health, a strongly validated child will respond simply to the alarm in our voice without demanding an explanation until later. But in a clearly non-threatening situation, the child finds even rare postponements difficult to tolerate, because there is the unanswered question of why the postponement? We must expect to have to explain the reasons for the postponement as well as the reason for the criticisms when the opportunity for explanation comes.

We need to postpone the explanation with a strong validating message if we hope to have the child wait willingly. Here are some possible ways. "Josh, I know you would like very much to understand why, but it is a private thing that we should talk about when we are at home (or alone)." "I feel silly asking you to stop when you don't know why, but I will explain it to you later when just the two of us can talk together."

Of course, it is preferable that these questions first come up in a private environment where we can give prompt explanations.

This is a good reason for encouraging the same courtesies within the family as are expected in public. However, if there are behaviors that do not make us uncomfortable but that we know may offend the general public, we need not impose the public's limitations on the family. Rather, with the expectation that our child will be receptive to useful information, we can inform him of the different behaviors appropriate for different environments. For example, if he chooses to run around with some toy poised as a penis, we can let it go for a minute and then say something like this: "That's funny but it's pretty silly. Most people consider penises private."

We must be wary of the principle of observation, though. If we go beyond imparting useful information, if we issue a warning, or even a strong instruction or wish, the child may well remember the behavior which she has observed will get an inordinate amount of our attention. If she senses that we are especially fearful of some relatively harmless public behavior, she may choose to display it deliberately some time when she is feeling unloved. Extra warnings can also make her suspect that we are uncaring about her, because we choose to place irrational limitations on her behavior when the situation has not even yet arisen.

The best complement, then, to offering neutral information in the privacy of our home is not extra warnings but rather our own example. If the child sees that we modify our behavior somewhat to accommodate the sensibilities of the general public, she is likely to imitate us.

For example, if I avoid kissing my spouse passionately in public, I need not be surprised when my child chooses not to hug me in front of his friends. Similarly, if I sit with my feet on the floor when there are guests, even though I put them up when only my family is around, the child is likely to do likewise, needing only a gentle reminder if he temporarily forgets that there are guests.

There is a great deal of literature on the role of early touching and affection in the child's future capacity to maintain a close, intimate human relationship, despite society's inhibitions about sexual contact. It is, therefore, critical that we sweep away any nagging fears that get in the way of our nurturing instincts toward our children. Studies have shown that mothers who have skin-to-skin contact with their newborn baby in the first twelve hours of the baby's life are statistically less likely to be physically abusive of the child later and are more likely to maintain eye contact with the child when they are interacting. These kinds of studies demonstrate that parental closeness is not the same as sexual aberration and may indeed discourage rather than encourage aberration. Again, we must trust that our best parenting instincts and the expressed needs of the child will operate in the interests of the survival and health of the child. In short, if we want to hug our child, it is our best chance to give a validating message at the highest level of abstraction. A hug is worth a thousand words.

We need to remind ourselves of the many levels of abstraction involved in every sexual or sensual interaction and in every communication on the subject. We all know the debate about love without sex and sex without love. Even that debate is primarily a question of levels of abstraction: Can human beings be satisfied with interactions at only one level of abstraction? The debate is unending.

But for purposes of our parenting, we can take comfort in our ability to guide our children toward the patterns of thinking which will best express their human potential. In our relationships with our children, we can communicate in a validating way at all levels: by the completely abstract sharing of spiritual energy between parent and child, by our declarations of "I love you," by our hugs, by our sincere, truthful answers to questions about how babies are born and what moms and dads do to make them and why girls and boys are different, by exemplary open signs of affection between parents, by our occasional touches of encouragement, by offering opportunities to observe normal sensuality such as allowing the two- or three-year-old to play in the bathroom when we are showering, and by accepting and validating the most precise level of the child's personal experience of his or her genitals.

With the ubiquitous exposure to sexual stimuli, suggestive humor, and nude and sexually explicit material in posters, movies, songs, MTV, video, arcades, magazines and more, parents may feel trapped by the dilemma of whether to isolate their children from the general culture or lose all control over their developing sexual identity, values, and attitudes.

But we can take heart that the most powerful influence on them is still us. It is not our opinions about sex, which we may harp on again and again to the point of boredom, but our attitudes and example toward our bodies, sex roles, authority, privacy, friendship, force, tenderness, and affection that will give our children the most guidance for their emerging sexuality.

If we are open about our feelings, try to live by our own values, admit it when we don't practice what we preach, and let them see our efforts to come to terms with our own confusion or ambiguity, this will be the strongest affirmation for a healthy attitude toward sex.

When a child's family life is confused and has gaps in these areas, he is most likely to latch on to aberrative behavior or fascinations outside the family.

It is worth noting also that we parents need not be afraid of speaking our minds about what we think of particular sexual behaviors, exploitation, public exposure, dress, innuendo, and so forth for fear of being unliberated or repressive. It is not our specific beliefs but how we share them that teaches the children whether to respect others' choices and stand up for their own or to bully or be bullied.

Without vague fears about our children, we can more easily make our judgments about what movies, shows, magazines, and so forth we are comfortable having our children experience at each stage of their growth. We need not despair about occasional exposure elsewhere if we are consistent and caring within the home environment over which we do have control.

Though our guidelines may not be embraced by the child, they can offer the child a welcome haven of reliability in an otherwise very confused area of our society. And an atmosphere of acceptance and nonjudgmental love makes the child comfortable bringing to us any questions or emerging options before she has committed herself to any dangerous or destructive course.

For every crazy teen we see on TV or in the movies, we

can usually think of one in the deli or down the street whose attitudes are just fine. There is plenty we can do to increase the odds that our child will resemble the latter.

It is worth considering the pop psychology concepts of the Oedipal complex and penis envy. These, like the anal and oral characters mentioned in the last chapter, were an important contribution of Freud. But like those character types, they are not inevitable pitfalls whose severity depends on a roll of the dice. We are free to guide our children toward a healthy accepting relationship with both parents. We do this by seeing to it that we set the best example we can without insincerity, by being open with our personal efforts to overcome useless stereotypes, and by making the effort to provide useful information and reasonable explanations for the multiple mysteries of sexual behavior.

By doing this, we can discard our fears of the unknowable goings on in the sexual consciousness of the child and instead act toward him with the same respect for his privacy and self-esteem that we try to extend to adults. We have then set good foundations for a joyful parent-child relationship which will eventually comfortably accommodate new sexual dimensions for the adolescent and emerging adult.

CHAPTER 7

Helping

ONE of the child's greatest pleasures can be helping her parents do things. It is the clearest opportunity to observe, imitate, and learn. Modern life creates a problem for helping, because unlike sorting seeds, herding goats, threading beads, carrying water, pulling vegetables, or hauling wood, many of the activities we spend our time on today do not lend themselves easily to child participation. Cooking on a range, typing, driving, running machines, writing checks, or reading newspapers are activities which are hard for children to help with. Because of this, it is important that when we do something with which our child could help, we take the time to let her help. At the same time, we need to make extra efforts to see that any helping the child does is a validating experience which reinforces the child's sense of her own competence. Otherwise, the frequent observation of adult activities in which she cannot participate or repeated failure at occasional attempts to help will encourage a sense of incompetence and helplessness.

When we want to include a child in an activity, it is often helpful to try to subdivide the activity. We can refine it into its component parts. Often a project which would otherwise seem too difficult to allow for a helping child can then include him in a way satisfying to him even if it seems surprisingly simple to us. For example, if we are making a pie for a dinner, the chore of putting the fruits in the bowl can be enough to occupy the child for quite a time, especially if he is left to do it his own way. From even the smallest task, a child can get a sense of participating, so long as his part in the overall project is clear and real.

We must remember that the desire to do the critical function in any activity is not necessarily a basic desire. The desire to be center stage is not necessarily inherent in children. So long as a child feels that she is spiritually center stage among her family —that is, adequately validated overall—she will not seek center stage all the time. Then cooperation is as satisfying as doing a whole project herself, perhaps even more so. Cooperation serves as a very effective means of external validation, while doing something by herself may require self-validating, unless she receives our sincere praise. Even then, praise of the thing done does not validate the person. The best validation of the person is praise which recognizes her feelings: "You must have had fun making such a complicated design with the vegetables," rather than "What a beautiful design you made."

When the child is helping, not only can we empathize with the child's sense of accomplishment, but we can express our gratitude, one of the most powerful validating mechanisms. If we can sincerely thank the child for her help (even if the job took three times as long as it would have otherwise), the child will get the high-level message that she is worthwhile, helpful, wanted, appreciated, loved.

It is also important that we allow our child the room to accept gratitude in a healthy way. He need not say, "Ah, it was nothing," when it was something. Rather, we want to encourage the child to value things at their worth at the appropriate level of abstraction. If we sincerely appreciate that Matt scraped three carrots for the evening salad, we want him to feel good about it. A healthier response from the child would be, "It was fun, Mom!" Or "I like to help." If the child is not used to this kind of exchange, we can even guide him: "I really appreciate your helping me. It is fun to work with you in the kitchen. You looked like you were enjoying it!" The child may well say, "Yes, I did," as he runs off to the next activity. Next time he will have some idea what he might say in response to our thanks.

It is especially hard for the less domestic parent to find activities to share with the child. And it is particularly hard too for any parent who works full time outside the home. The parent may well be inclined just to "groove" with the child, or to try to do special childhood activities which the parent imagines the child will like. But unless that parent has very reinforcing things to say, and unless the child is sure that the parent enjoys the childhood activity as much as she does, it is important, too, that the parent do something with the child which the child perceives to be important to the parent. Licking stamps, turning newspaper pages, pointing to the words as the parent reads a bedtime book, carrying the garbage bag when baskets are dumped, turning on the television, carrying out the dishes, or any other small task can say a lot about our confidence, respect, and love for the child.

We need to recognize, however, that a different message emerges if we let the child serve us rather than help us. Such things as the classic getting the slippers is not helping in the constructive sense we mean here. Likewise, in our constant hurry, if we see the child doing something capably, we are often tempted to leave her and go on to something else. The helping aspect is lost then, too, and so is the positive message to the child. The situation then resembles the case when the child does something herself. The most we can do is empathize after the activity is over. We have not shared the activity—the process of helping—itself.

Another important aspect of helping is trust and guidance. We need to give the child time to come up with his own ways of doing things or solutions to problems as often as we can. If the child is working on one portion of a project while we work on another, we should stay close enough to be in tune with the problems or limitations the child is encountering, so that we can offer information or answer requests for suggestions without appearing to be checking up on him or worrying about whether he will "do it right."

Most of us know how nervous and awkward we can get if we are being watched by someone we fear who expects that we might fail. Some people thrive on this kind of tension. Most become miserably handicapped. But there is no denying that the tension is there. Unless a child has already developed a defensive mechanism which steels his will in the presence of a disbeliever, he is more likely to make mistakes if we expect him to. Frequent mistakes will eventually persuade him that he deserves low esteem. Therefore, we need to show, by the way in which we lend a guiding hand, that we have confidence in his ability.

Most of us have a vision of those people who achieve best when they must prove their ability to skeptics. But they are seldom happy achievers. They rarely feel contentment in their work, but only in making fools of the skeptics. The happy achiever is one who had the trust of his parents in his formative years, and who was able to internalize that trust, so that as an adult, he can do what he wants without regard to whether others think he can do it and without any ulterior motives relating to those opinions. Achieving against odds is not the same as achieving in order to beat the odds. In fact, whether the tasks our children choose to undertake as adults are helpful or meaningless to their communities may well depend on which of these attitudes the children have adopted.

Let us take joy in the help of our children and be openly grateful for it.

CHAPTER 8

Playing

W E often consider playing the particular province of children. We all know what it is but are hard put to define it. Psychologists try to describe its aspects in different ways, but all agree that it is essential to the learning process of human children. Since interpretation and imitation are so central to human learning, activities which mimic observations of the world in a low-risk environment are very useful to the child. Play usually involves these elements. The child engages in activities which mimic the activities which he has observed. Meanwhile, the activities are limited in space, time, materials, and people, so as to minimize any real risk of harm. The activities may be very realistic, such as ironing doll clothes or arguing about who will go through the door first. The activities may be very fanciful, such as being a fish caught in a castle or singing a song about a trip to the moon. All are based on interpretations of things the child has observed in his life. Usually they refer to recent observations, but if something has remained mysterious to the child, it may crop up at any time until the mystery is resolved.

In many ways play is like dreams. It allows a person to act

out almost any idea with none of the consequences of translating the idea into real life. It serves as a harmless way to integrate experience into one's store of information for future use. It allows one to test what the likely consequences of an action are without actually experiencing them. In this light, it seems natural that children should play a good deal more than adults. They are learning so much more each day than any adult! We may marvel at a would-be traveler who learns a language in a week, or a physicist who memorizes hundreds of formulae for a doctoral examination. But no matter how many bits of information an adult can absorb, the child's information stream is likely to beat it. When we contemplate how many different levels of abstraction a child is observing and potentially learning at one time, the challenge seems awesome.

It is no wonder then that the reviewing, cataloguing, and filing which go on in dreams and which are sufficient to integrate the new knowledge of adults is not enough to meet the needs of the healthy, learning child.

If we appreciate this need to play, to act out observations, and to try out interpretations, we can also trust that the child is the best judge of what kind of play she needs at any given time. If we tend to feel guilty about not being able to think up wonderful games for our children, we need to let go of that guilt. Our role in play is merely to see that the children have enough stimuli around them to engage their minds in playful examination of their observations and experience. A child may need redirection from time to time when one particular mode of play is exhausted. But usually when a healthy child can think of nothing to do it is either because she needs some positive input at more abstract levels, such as any kind of loving attention from the parent, or she is ready to sleep.

Sometimes keeping hands off the choice of play is very difficult. If the children are quarreling but unite against me when I interfere to "make peace," most likely they are playing out some scenario of a quarrel they have observed. Often, if we are conscious of this kind of play, we will even recognize the quarrel as one we parents engaged in last night or last week. If not that, then it may be one they saw on television recently or one they saw between the grandparents last month which particularly gave them food for thought.

That these incidents were observed should not concern us so much as that they occurred in the first place. Since they are bound to occur sometimes, it is most important that the children be allowed to work them out healthfully through play as long as they need to.

This is not to say that we cannot guide the play, without interfering with it. If we learn by observing our children's play that they are trying hard to figure out some sexual stereotype, for example, we can wait for some interpretative play and then add some information which will allow the children to interpret more accurately.

Suppose the children have seen a Humphrey Bogart film on television. The daughter says something like: "You don't love me. You're only using me." The son says, "Women are all alike," and turns away. If we can, we should do our best to identify the source of the model. This way we do not have to develop a dissertation on sex roles. We need only help interpret the precise observation. "Oh, I see that you remember that movie we saw on television the other day. Wasn't that strange the way the man thought the woman couldn't think the way he did? They were having a lot of trouble understanding how they felt about each other. A lot of adventure movies have people act that way." The parent has validated the children's capabilities in remembering and trying to interpret the observation. Then he has helped the children distinguish the observation from their other experience by identifying the context as an adventure movie and an example of people doing a poor job of sharing their feelings.

The more difficult case is when we cannot identify the source. We can ask the source, but we must do so in a way which does not threaten the child's perception of her freedom to play with any observation at all. If this seems too difficult in a given case, the best we can do is comment upon how strange, different, odd, or silly the behavior is, but only after we have said something which acknowledges the value of the child's play. We might say, "That sounds like some argument!" Or, "You really look angry when you say that!" Then we can say something like, "People

who love each other don't usually think of each other that way."
Whatever we say, it is worthwhile remembering that our primary
purpose is to reinforce the prior experience of the child in the
face of the most recent challenge. Another way of looking at it
is as reinforcement of the correct abstract interpretation of the
recent observation. But above all, we must keep intact the even
more abstract message that the children are free to play out their
learning experiences.

Of course, most children's play is not so negative. It is often
strongly reinforcing of the best of their experience. It may be very
cooperative, mimic the kinds of exercises the children enjoy at
school, or relive the most fun experiences of the family. Whatever
the play, parents are free not only to play with the child when
invited, but to cherish the brilliance of the play mechanism and
the unself-conscious moments of childhood we are able to observe.

As with other activities, we must examine the influence that
our example can have on play. What kind of example can parents
set for play? Many of us have forgotten how to play all but the
most formal games.

Formal games generally have many preordained limits and
a very precise level of focus. But their fun still comes from the
other levels of abstraction (such as when a quiet, giving father
becomes suddenly amusingly acquisitive in a monopoly game),
and from the flights of fancy beyond the narrow limitations (one
can become a king twice over in a mere checkers game). So even
the most formal game is worth playing with your child.

If you wish to go a bit beyond the formal games, the next
step is to make up your own rules. Or let the children make them
up as you go along. The very young child cares very little who
wins in the end. Likewise, he seldom cares whether the rules are
consistent throughout the game. It is worth trying to allow for
this kind of flexibility as we parents try to expand our capacity
for play. It gives us some release from always trying to control
and keep consistent all aspects of our lives. It also helps us rebuild
our faith that even without strict rules people who love each other
and are willing to give and take can have a very good time
together. It also gives us, not to mention our children, the broad-

ening experience of having them make rules for us! (If someone is going to make rules for us when we are old, wouldn't we like most for it to be our children?)

For parents who are more adventurous in play, it is still important to let the children lead. For example, if the children want to make puppets, we should let them decide how, rather than imposing our own craft skills on them in a well-meaning effort to "make the puppets work better." On the other hand, if the child asks us how to make the beard look real or how to attach the hands or some other precise question, then we can answer gladly.

Often when we are tempted to take over a child's play, we are reliving a time when our parents did the same thing to us. After thirty years, we may still want to do a particular craft ourselves. Should we perpetuate this pattern so that we only get to express our craft skills when we are adults? Even when we are invited to demonstrate a skill, then, we must be careful not to take over the project so that the children become spectators or become disappointed with their product because it does not look as nice or neat as ours.

Another important way to engage in play with the children is to allow ourselves to be silly. For example, if we recognize a set of roles which the children are acting out, we can assume an appropriate role ourselves and enjoy a good validating laugh. But we should never stay involved longer than a moment, again so that the children will not feel that we are changing the nature of their play. If they ask us to participate, that's fine; but still we should not do it too often.

In general, we should accept childish silliness and exuberance as a form of play. We need not treat noise or bouncing on beds as an all-or-nothing proposition. Rather, we can accept it as an expression of joy and let it go for a while and then set reasonable limits on it.

Sibling arguments are often a way of playing with ways of resolving conflicts. It is an interesting way for us to find out what patterns they are learning. It is important not to impose ourselves as peacemakers too often, or this learning experience will be stifled.

Play is much more enjoyable for parents when we don't feel that we have some particular lesson in mind whenever we play with the children. We can be content to know that they are learning and that they are working on the lessons that they are most eager to know and therefore most likely to learn.

It is worth mentioning that this child-led approach to play has definite implications for the kind of instruction which purports to teach through play. No one but the person who plays knows what level he is going to learn on or what he wants most to learn at any time. If a child is playing and a teacher directs the child in a specific direction because there is a specific skill which the teacher has in mind, that interference will carry with it the negative messages which parental interference threatened, as discussed above. The child may or may not learn the skill, but the limitations on the child's freedom to play and the apparent lack of confidence of the teacher in the child's leadership will have consequences beyond the particular skill. Most likely, the self-motivated child who is free to play will pick up the particular skill very easily whenever he perceives a need for it.

The instruction program, then, that hopes to give children a head start by tricking them into learning something before they perceive the need may very well be teaching more serious abstract lessons of low self-esteem, conformity, and inadequacy, which none of us want to encourage. Also, since children are such acute observers, we may even find that they begin to distrust teachers early on, because they see that the teacher is trying to teach them one thing by having them do another. If learning must be camouflaged as play, they may ponder, perhaps learning is not fun.

It seems better to let the child know when the parent or teacher thinks he should learn something he would not otherwise learn just now, and leave play to the child himself, as his own unique, creative way to learn what he wants to know.

CHAPTER 9

Learning

LEARNING is a constant activity of children and a most important one. Everything they see and do adds to their perception of themselves and the world around them. Many of the operating principles relate directly to the child's innate capability to learn. The child's keen observation, receptivity, tendency to imitate, desire to please, and ability to interpret on different levels of abstraction are all inborn qualities which help the child learn. We must assume that the main function of the superb capacity of humans to learn is to make the child fit to survive in her environment and to continue her species successfully. Human beings do not have the short life spans of some creatures, which enable them to evolve genetically to adapt to changing environments. Nor do we have a neat set of genetically transmitted instinctual behaviors which adapt us to a relatively safe environmental niche. Instead of these, we have an amazing capacity to adapt as individuals through learning and an equally amazing capacity to pass on this kind of adaptation through teaching. The genetic capacity of our children to learn predisposes them to be receptive to our teaching.

If learning is so basic an activity of children, why is it that so often we have trouble getting our children to pay attention to what we say, to mind our warnings, to do their homework, to listen to the teacher, to take an interest in reading, to keep an open mind to new learning?

The way we teach and the way we respond to the child's learning may make the difference between a child who seems to put up his guard when anyone tries to teach him anything, and the child who is a "sponge" for learning. The operating principles serve as a guide in any learning or teaching situation.

The operating principle of trust is always a good place to begin. Do we act toward our children as if we trusted them to want to learn? If we accept that learning is in the interest of the child, we must also accept that in general the child will choose to learn, because, according to the principle of trust, we know that he will generally act in his own best interest. We must assume then that every child has a basic desire to learn and experiences joy in learning.

But why doesn't this basic desire manifest itself all the time? Actually it does. Do we tend to assume that we have control over what our children learn? If we accept that the child learns from observation and imitation as well as from his desire to please (that is, doing as he is told), we must also accept that we do not have control over what a child learns in any given situation, because no matter what we intend, the child listens and learns at the most abstract level first. If the child has not already accumulated enough experience to give him useful knowledge at the more abstract levels, he will be slow to learn at the more precise levels.

For example, if we try to teach the multiplication tables to Mitchell and he does not yet have the more abstract message that he is able to learn, he may have serious difficulty. Or if he has trouble with the even more abstract level of whether he is a worthwhile person, he may spend all his time trying to determine whether his friends are impressed with him. In that case, if his friends appear amused by his being flippant about his lessons, he may actually resist learning the tables. Nevertheless, he is learning. He is learning that in his group resisting precise learning brings approval. We might ask why would he not seek the approval of his teacher first? The more validating the style of teaching, the more likely the child will be to look to the teacher for approval. In Mitchell's situation, it is likely that classmates have shown him more love—that is, unconditional approval—than has the teacher.

If we accept that we do not have control over the level of abstraction at which the child seeks to learn in any given situation, we need not despair of any control. Rather, our role is to guide the child in her learning. We are uniquely suited as parents to recognize and address gaps in knowledge at the more abstract levels of learning. We can help make our children supremely receptive to precise learning merely by seeing that their abstract learning has been sound. We are released from the responsibility to know everything before they do, to learn the new math, or whatever, before they do. Our task, instead, is to give them the most solid background in abstract learning that we can.

First, we can make sure that they get the basic validation of love they need. This is the most abstract and essential learning: If a child does not perceive herself as worthwhile, we cannot expect her to direct her powers toward survival and adaptation. The next more precise step will be to give the child confidence that she can learn whatever she needs to. Many examples in this book illustrate how to show this confidence.

At the next level of learning the child needs appreciation. Praise shows our appreciation, but it must be used with care. We need to address praise to the efforts of the child as much as or more than to his particular products. We must be especially wary of saying that everything a child does is fantastic, wonderful, and perfect. Exaggerated praise can be as bad as no praise at all. Because children observe everything and are sensitive to very abstract levels as well as to precise ones, they sense very quickly when we are not being genuine or when we are applying different standards to them than we apply to ourselves or to others. If the child senses the inaccuracy of the parent's assessment, he will tend to doubt that his activities have any real value, since there is no way for him to assess where the truth ends and the exaggeration begins. The child may then be constantly seeking parental attention and approval, showing off, and appearing very capable but at the same time very dependent on the parent's presence for his strength. The child may also respond by acting very competitive, because he seeks constantly to compare himself with others in order to persuade himself that he is indeed superior and that the parent is indeed telling the truth. If we find that our praise has been disproportionate to the activities we have been praising, the best approach is to refocus our praise to a higher level of abstraction. Although the child's painting may not be the greatest in the world and we should not therefore tell him that it is, we do love him as much as anyone can love anyone, and this we can tell him. We can say, "My, you must have worked hard on that painting. I like it. It is so colorful and bright," instead of "What a fantastic painting!"

Often families who find themselves reluctant to express their love with physical tenderness or direct assertions of love are prone to exaggerated praise at more precise levels. When we understand what we are doing, a gradual adjustment of our behavior will gradually free our children of self-doubt and allow them to develop the confidence they need.

Having considered what the operating principles imply for how our children learn, we should look at their implications for prevailing methods of schooling. We shall consider three topics here: when to begin schooling; how to overcome the negative implications of tests; and how to guide learning through peer pressure.

The time to begin schooling is, of course, when the child is ready for it. But that time is difficult to determine until we know what "it" is. What is school, from the point of view of an essentially spiritual being? Most of the discussion in this book centers on activities at home among the child's immediate relatives and friends. How does school fit in?

From the point of view of society, the school serves two purposes. It assures that each child has at least a minimal capability for precise tasks which will be necessary for the child to function on her own in society. It also supplements and sometimes substitutes for the parents as a socializing force, by reinforcing in the child the prevailing value system of our culture. With these two major focal points, the schools necessarily put the most time into teaching precise skills and behaviors. They do not focus on the abstract learning which we have been most concerned with in this book.

If modern schooling does not focus on the more abstract levels of learning and if we trust that our children will seek to learn so long as they have received adequate validation in the early years, then there would seem to be no reason to rush the children off to school. Of course, there are many practical reasons to consider it. Both parents may feel the need to work outside the home and after a certain age, school seems more attractive than a sitter. "At least she will be learning something." Or we may live in a neighborhood that offers little peer interaction for our children. "I want him to learn to get along with others." Or we want her to have a head start on schooling. We may feel that education is the key to success and happiness, and we are convinced that the sooner it begins the better. Parents often toss these considerations around painfully for a long time with no sense of guidance toward a final decision. Even when we finally decide, we have periodic self-doubts and if something seems wrong, we tend to wonder if our decision was sound.

For this kind of decision we need to put first things first. Of course, we must think of what is good for us. An unhappy parent, one who feels victimized either by family life or by the outside world, can hardly give a child the positive validation that is needed. But we can also keep our minds clear about the needs of the child. Most important, she needs the love of those closest to her. Mary cannot learn to get along with others well if she has no opportunity to get along with her family and if she has no chance to observe in her family examples of how one gets along with another. Perhaps a sitter would be better than early schooling if the sitting environment offers a substitute family. This may well be more what the child needs than acceleration of the school experience.

Similarly, ambitions we may have for our child to have a head start on education may well be separate from his needs. If we trust that a happy, well-validated child will be drawn to a musical instrument if that is what will make him happy, it may well be better to solidify that background of love than to start the violin lessons early. How often we hear of people who never considered a career in music because they hated those early piano lessons. They did not hate music. They only missed the strong validating experience of running around outside with one's friends making innumerable harmless decisions all on one's own and therefore felt inadequate as musicians.

How can we ever take on the responsibility of deciding, when our children are four years old, whether they will be mathematicians, concert violinists, building contractors, or nurses? Instead of assuming this impossible responsibility, we can do what comes much more naturally. We can encourage our children in any constructive activity of their choice and continue to give positive validation at the most essential spiritual level. It is ironic that many of the new wave schools which profess to produce geniuses in particular subjects may owe their success less to the immersion in precise intellectual or manual tasks than to the fact that the parents almost always are intimately involved in the constant encouragement the children receive.

If we can separate our needs from those of our children and consider our priorities for both, we can have confidence that we are making the best decision we can about when to start school.

We usually assume that testing is an unavoidable part of school. How else can a teacher know if he is getting through? Parents don't feel compelled to test their children. That is because we know our children so well. We trust our own perceptions of their progress. But a large public school system supported with public funds can hardly afford to rely on the individual impressions of its teachers. Different teachers may have different impressions of the same situations. Besides, the school is most interested in precise skills and behaviors, many of which do lend themselves to fairly objective testing. But how well do children lend themselves to testing? Does a child who does not take tests well promise to contribute less to society than one who tests well?

The mere act of testing suggests that it is possible for the child not to have learned the lesson. If there were not two alternatives, we would not need a test. But the operating principles show that a child feels every doubt and question we may raise about her value, even if for a moment. Perhaps the preoccupation nof our schools with tests is giving a subtle but constant message to our children that we do not trust them, that they may be incompetent, and that we expect a certain proportion of them to be failing at learning.

If we parents recognize this subtle influence of schools, there are several things we can do. We can try to choose schools which do their best to minimize this message, either by fewer tests or by actively giving positive validation to counterbalance the effects of tests. We can actively try to eliminate from our schools unnecessary tests and try to "humanize" the schools by training our teachers to offer more validation at the abstract levels. We can encourage schools to put off testing programs until the children are old enough to grasp the fact that tests do not bring their essential worth into question but only their most recent precise learning.

In addition to these efforts, we can begin at home to counteract any negative messages from the testing at school.

We can avoid any testing at home. We should avoid putting our children in the position of having to prove themselves. Instead, we can act according to the operating principles, guiding them by example, by careful explanation, by referencing to the most important aspect of any situation. We can actively express our trust and love.

In addition, we can guide our children directly in their attitude toward school and testing. This may be hardest of all. If a six-year-old gets half of his lesson marked "wrong," we will be hard-pressed not to show our disappointment. We must work hard to overcome in ourselves the feeling that someone has judged him deficient. But we should work through those feelings between ourselves and muster our strength to say to the child something like this: "Oh, you missed a lot of these. You must have been in a hurry when you did them," or "These must have been hard to do. I guess you worked a long time on them." Surprisingly, the child will usually tell you exactly why he had a problem. This is quite different from the usual conversation:

"Susan, you missed half of these problems!"
"Dad, I hate arithmetic!"
"Oh, come on. You shouldn't hate it."

At this point, a father can feel very helpless and frustrated. Instead, he can turn even a failure into a validating experience by seeing the good in it: the efforts the child must have made, the distractions she must have faced, the disappointment she must have sensed at not having done what was expected of her.

We might be concerned that all we are doing is offering the child excuses. But in practice, we hear excuses only when the child is put on the defensive. In fact, if we respond in a validating way but have suggested the wrong excuse, we may very well hear something like this: "I wasn't in a hurry. I just don't understand division. But Jessica is trying to teach me."

We may feel that we are sabotaging the efforts of the school if we don't withhold our approval when the child fails. But if we think through the operating principles, we can see that this is a false fear. If a child fails in a precise task, it will do little good to indicate to her that she is also a failure at a more abstract level. The child has the courage to try again at the precise task exactly because she is confident of her self-worth and ability. Unconditional love from the family is the easiest way to foster that courage.

Finally, if we sense that our children are interpreting tests as judgments on their essential worth, we must help them understand the tests at the appropriate level of abstraction. We might say something like, "You feel very disappointed with that paper. You tried very hard, but you did not do as well as the teacher expected. Sometimes when you do badly, you feel as if you're just no good at all."

When we articulate the child's feelings, instead of saying that he shouldn't feel that way, he is more likely to hear our message correctly. He will be able to recognize that his response may be too deep, instead of becoming defensive about his feelings.

While this kind of parental comment may seem very alien at first, with practice it becomes clear that we can successfully infuse an emotionally trying time with some important validation for our child. And we can do so without the child feeling that we have been condescending or passed judgment on his emotions. Rather, we have effectively helped the child interpret a major element in a major part of his life—that is, tests in school.

The operating principles also offer significant guidance in helping our children fend off negative peer pressure. Most of us feel that peer interaction in school is a positive thing for our children. But we fear mightily the real risks of strong influences in the direction of experimentation with sex, cigarettes, drugs, and alcohol. We may also have to contend with daughters who want to be too thin, sons who want to cut their hair strangely, or numerous other more or less negative effects of peers. All of these, in one form or another, have plagued youth in every highly organized society. The fact is that many youths do survive the period of exposure with no permanent harm and a strong sense of responsibility to themselves. To increase the chances that our child will be among these, we can do two things.

First, we can see that our child has predominantly validating experiences through his youth. This kind of upbringing makes the child less vulnerable to the powerful attractions of validation by the group, the gang, the kids. It also preserves a strong parent-child relationship, so that the child will be more likely to share difficult choices with the parent before he has committed himself.

Second, we can actively guide the child toward a healthy attitude about peer pressure. Our own example is probably the single most powerful lesson in attitude. Do we dress to please our crowd? Do we smoke when everyone else does, or drink when everyone else does? Do our decisions sound like they depend a lot on what the neighbors or our friends will think?

How do we handle jibing comments? Do we act weak and defensive, or do we assert our free choice and offer no excuses but our own well-considered preference? Our example can give our children the skills they need to respond to peer pressure in a way that allows them to maintain their self-respect and often the respect of their peers.

In addition to example, we can discuss the influences on the child with her. We can explain how we feel about drugs, sex outside of long-term commitment, getting drunk, or smoking. The child will listen so long as we are genuine about our feelings, avoid double standards without a real reason, and avoid giving the child the impression that her solution has to be the same as ours. By referencing the child, we can avoid telling the child what to do when she faces us with an impossible dilemma:

CHILD: "If I don't drink at Judy's party, the other kids will think I'm no fun to be with!"

PARENT: "You want the other kids to think that you are fun to be with."

CHILD: "Sure. But they get so drunk, they really aren't any fun."

PARENT: "Sometimes they disgust you when they go too far."

CHILD: "Yeah. Maybe I can just hang out with the quiet ones at the party."

If this scenario sounds unbelievable, we must call on the principle of trust. If we are good listeners, if we validate whatever feelings we hear our children express, we can trust that they will have the strength to face their problems themselves. Then, they are more likely to come up with solutions, even better than we could have thought of, since we are not in their shoes nor do we have all their information. Also, they will have made the decision themselves and are therefore more likely to be happy with it.

School is a challenge. It does not substitute for the parent. In fact it renders the parent's role all the more important, because of the extra challenges the child faces. Parents can nevertheless enjoy the experience if they guide the child with care so that the school experience is a positive one.

CHAPTER 10

Socializing

HUMAN beings are by nature social creatures. They enjoy eating together, sleeping together, traveling together, working together, playing together, and sharing thoughts together. Children continually demonstrate the need to be with people. Even the shy child will want to watch from a distance rather than be removed altogether from a group of people. For the adult, the desire to socialize serves a number of purposes. In evolutionary terms, it makes for more reliable feeding, more reliable shelter, and stronger defense from predators. It also makes possible the learning processes we considered in the last chapter—learning processes which have apparently made possible the amazing success of our species. Our spiritual consciousness, which has made us greater masters of our destiny than is any other creature, develops when we see our beings reflected in our social contacts with others.

The child is even more dependent on a willingness to be with people. The child is wholly dependent on others for his basic needs. In addition, the child can learn very little without social interaction. And since learning is the child's principal activity and is essential to his survival, Nature has given the child a powerful urge to seek out and respond to people.

Sometimes we find this social impulse both disarming and frightening. The child will accept almost anything from other people. At the same time, that is the kind of trust we wish we too felt comfortable in extending to other people. But we tend to conclude that we know better, that there are a lot of bad people in the world, and that the child must be taught to be wary. On the other hand, we want our children to know and seek the value of friendship and to be loyal and trusting toward those who are trustworthy. How can we accomplish all this?

In this chapter we can take a look at three kinds of social interaction: with siblings, with friends, and with strangers.

Parents are frequently frustrated by tension between siblings. We hear about sibling "rivalry" and feel that we must resign ourselves to inevitable tension in the household. The operating principles shed some important light on sibling relations.

First of all, we must trust that the sibling relationship is part of the human life plan and must necessarily have the potential to be a positive experience overall. The sibling is the third most influential person in a child's life. There can be no reason why this person should be a source of pain or animosity to the child. If we view sibling interactions as play in preparation for all future human interaction, we can begin to put in perspective the patterns of behavior that we see.

A constructive sibling relationship begins before the younger one is born. The expectant sibling will tend to adopt the attitude toward the new baby which his parents expect him to adopt. If we assume that he will feel displaced in our affections, we may try to reassure him that this will not happen. He may hear that it will not happen, but he will also hear the message at the more abstract level that we expect that it may happen.

Instead, we must concentrate on building the feelings we want, rather than guarding against the feelings we don't want. Then the child will not hear any secondary, unwanted messages. If we present the new baby as a further validation of love, the child will have ample room for the new one in his heart. A new sibling is a strong validation for him, if we think about it: If we did not enjoy the first, we would be less likely to want or have another. Also, we parents must feel secure enough with our older child that we are ready to take on another. All these positive feelings can be discussed with the older child. He will be surprisingly receptive. As long as we speak of our own feelings and try not to second-guess his, we will find that he will speak openly of anything troubling him. Then, instead of introducing problems by trying to avoid them, we can deal directly with any ones that actually arise.

Even if siblings have gotten off to a bad start, it is never too late to guide them toward a more positive relationship. We can set an example for them in getting along with others, we can trust them to work out their difficulties, we can remember to reference them to the more important elements in any situation, and we can help them interpret what they observe of themselves. One of the most common parental frustrations is the thankless task of being policeman, judge, and punisher all in one. We feel that we must always be on the lookout for conflict, must be ready to determine who was right and who was wrong, and must then punish or control the wrong-doer and sympathize with the right-doer.

In fact, this kind of intervention is the very last choice for solving sibling disputes. Just like resort to a court of law in adult affairs, it is at best only a partial solution to a conflict. It tends to leave wounds which may be as deep as or deeper than the original hurt. And like an adult lawsuit, it is appropriate only after all other methods of compromise or conflict resolution have failed. Having parental interference or going before a judge is only the last resort before people turn to violence. It is no substitute for handling the dispute by cooperation.

When our children seem about to come to blows, we need not feel that we must know exactly how the dispute arose or who is in the wrong. In the context of most sibling disputes, no one has really done anything wrong in an absolute sense. It is usually a matter of interpersonal manipulation, teasing, goading, provocation. If we approach the problem as a problem shared by both siblings, we do not need to play judge. In fact, we can start in very slowly.

PARENT: "Hey, kids, I'm hearing too much angry noise!"
SUSIE: "Well, Miranda took my bear!"
PARENT: "You are mad because Miranda has your bear. See if you can talk quietly to her about it."
MIRANDA: "But I had it first and Susie wasn't playing with it!"
PARENT: "You were enjoying the bear and you're mad that Susie wants it when you have it. I think you both can work this out."

It can be amazing how quickly the children can come to a solution, if we define the problem and then toss it gently back into their laps. Often their solution is one we never would have thought of. "You hold the bear while I feed him," or "Let's go play marbles and teach the bear too!" Usually their solution will have nothing to do with who wronged whom in the original conflict. Rather, it will tend to reflect momentary fears, needs, or feelings of the children which were altogether too subtle for us to placate by some formal intervention and judgment.

Using this approach, we have not had to plead for "sharing" and have avoided imposing any negative connotations on that pleasant activity. In addition, the children have experienced a strong validation. We have acknowledged their feelings, even less desirable ones like being mad. They have acknowledged each others' feelings and needs. And they have cooperated with each other. Cooperation generates a strong sense of spiritual identity because it takes two equals to cooperate.

There is an easy way to recognize when we are interfering too often in a judge-like way. If when we investigate a turmoil we frequently hear these protestations, we should rethink our approach:

"He did it!"
"I didn't do it."

"It wasn't me."
"She started it."

Any persistent use of "should" also suggests the need to return to the operating principles. "Nelly shouldn't push people." "Rene shouldn't keep me awake." "You should lock Tom in his room." "Beatrice shouldn't be allowed to go to the movies." All these suggest that the child is trying to apply rules to get her way. The child is anticipating that you will be judge and that you will want to label one side right and the other wrong. The children start to sound like little trial lawyers.

Aside from the dangers of substituting our judgments for their cooperation, it is easier if parents avoid a proliferation of rules which deal with nonessential behavior. If we have too many rules which do not relate to a real risk of harm to someone, we are likely to be easily manipulated or embarrassed when the child can name a rule to justify any behavior she wishes, or when the loser in a dispute can show us that we have applied the rule inconsistently. Rather, in the vast majority of situations, we should guide the children to develop a resolution for themselves.

We can expect our children to model their relationships with other people on the attitudes and patterns we use to guide them in their relationships with each other. Rather than encourage the casting of blame, the meting out of punishment, and the manipulation of guilt, we want to foster caring recognition of others' feelings and cooperative resolution of differences.

Children who are tired, hungry, or at a low ebb of self-esteem will tend to bicker more among themselves. Rather than fear a sudden onslaught of sibling rivalry, parents must recognize these needs, get through the immediate conflict with the least scarring, and meet the needs as soon as possible. Usually the would-be rivalry will disappear.

How we resolve disputes between ourselves will be a powerful model for how our children behave. If we have had a less than cordial interchange, we should not be surprised to see it mimicked within a day or two. Rather than set down a rule that we ourselves have already broken, it will be far more helpful to say something like: "You sound very mad. I get that way sometimes too. But I try hard not to say nasty things. I try to work things out. I would like you to try to do that too."

Our example is probably the most powerful influence on how our children relate to friends as well. If we appreciate friendships and create opportunities to share our thoughts, experiences, and traditions with friends, our children will want to do likewise. It is important that we acknowledge that our children's friends are as important to them as our friends are to us, in order to reinforce their adoption of these values. In view of the importance of imaginative play as well as of unstructured interaction with others, we should take care to entertain our children's friends as freely as we do our own.

While we want our children to be open to friendships, we need to trust their timing and interest. Many children who are allowed just to watch will be more likely to be more comfortable in relationships later than children who are forced into participatory activities before they are ready. We must also be careful not to give conflicting messages about other people. We cannot expect our children to be open to new friendships if we are in the habit ourselves of finding fault with our friends or new acquaintances. Our messages about strangers can be especially confusing.

We all want our children to be safe from evil-meaning strangers. But should we question their basic trust in people by warning them that strangers may be evil? The operating principle of abstraction instructs us that the child will interpret things on the most abstract level first. A child must reach a certain level of maturity and understanding before such a warning will not tend to bring into doubt trust of all people. In a sense, the child must be allowed to learn the basic rule that people are approachable, before we show him the exception, that some people are dangerous. Otherwise, he may conclude that nasty people are the rule rather than the exception.

As with so many other difficult lessons for children, it is the behavior we should focus on, not the motivation, when we wonder how to share what we know. If we fill our young child with a fear of strangers, is he going to be less vulnerable to evil-doers? He may merely be more fearful and therefore more vulnerable.

Though it seems to take a great deal more time at first, perhaps it is easier and safer in the long run to avoid unfocused fears and to accept a parental duty to protect our child absolutely in the first few years. Then when he is old enough to be able to behave cautiously in certain precise situations without picking up vague fears, we can describe the necessary behaviors to him.

By that time, he will probably have some idea already of how to handle himself, because he will have been with us in a variety of situations involving strangers. Meanwhile, it is our job to see that the child is always in the care of someone we trust with his life.

We may fear that waiting until the child is old enough to comprehend the precise threats in life will jeopardize the child's need to be on her own, making her own decisions and being out of a parent's sight. But a sense of self-worth does not depend on being independent. It depends only upon a sense of control over that which is in one's control. If the child is too young to understand the complexities of the modern world, it is our duty as parents to keep watch a little longer than we would have had to in a simpler world. Our chief concern must be that the core spiritual strength of our child will be secure.

These examples of socializing illustrate that no social lessons will be learned before their time. We parents can take comfort in the knowledge that open participation by our child in the social events of the family, and careful attention to her expressed needs for expansion of that social circle, will be most effective in fostering happy social patterns for her.

CHAPTER 11

Working

WE usually do not think of children working until we send them to school and they bring home homework. But their attitude toward work develops before they go to school and comes primarily from our example. Have we acted as if play is fun but work is not fun? Have we indicated that work is for adults and that children must enjoy being children while they can, or on the other hand that children should be eager to join the adult world of work? Are any or all of these messages the ones we want our children to hear?

Working involves even more complex attitudes. Do we act as if the work we do at home is drudgery while the work we do away from home is challenging and important? Do we feel that we are wasting our time when we help our child clean up his room but that we are acting constructively when we stay late at work? Do we act as if raising children is all work and no play?

Whether or not these are attitudes we want or expect our children to have, we must be conscious that we have control over whether we encourage or discourage them in our children. We often hear how ironic it is that children will mimic work in their play only to resist work when it becomes a real obligation. It seems likely, though, that we parents give enough unthinking messages to encourage this attitude. We may find that we often express the wish to be doing something other than some task we consider an obligation. Children cannot be expected to overcome strong examples merely by force of commands: "Take pleasure in your chores! You have to do them no matter what anyhow."

A child who has known work only in this context will likely seek adult work which is uninteresting and programmed by somebody else. In contrast, if we want our children to be drawn to work that takes initiative and self-discipline, we must allow them the freedom to use their own initiative to plan their time and their means for accomplishing tasks. We must also have faith that if children feel validated by their smaller achievements, they will develop the self-discipline to take on larger ones. We should ask our children, then, to do no more than they can do with a positive attitude.

We may feel that this is unrealistic. Most of the jobs in the world are not challenging, we might think, so most of the children should be prepared to do work purely out of a sense of obligation. We should remind ourselves, however, that there are executives making exciting, important decisions who still consider their work drudgery, while there are bus-drivers who take great pride and pleasure in their work. We need to let go of the awesome responsibility of trying to second-guess our child's future and to prepare her for a certain role. Instead, we can help the child take an attitude toward work which allows her to take pleasure in her work, whatever it may be.

Probably the most complex problems with respect to the working activities of the child relate to two-career families. What attitude toward work will a child have who feels he is missing his parents because of their jobs? On the other hand, what kind of validation is available to a child whose mother has a low opinion of herself because she is not "out there doing something productive"? Whatever the patterns of work which we choose, we should take special care to see that the children understand how we feel about it. If we feel better about ourselves by contributing to public life as well as to our family life, we can tell the children so, no matter how young they are. The principle of receptivity indicates that they can understand often a lot more than we give them credit for.

But the less actual time we spend with our children, the stronger the validating influence of those times must be. The working parent must be especially careful that any interaction with the child gives the right messages at the most abstract levels first. For example, the working mother or father who has only a limited time to go over a second-grader's school work with her may think it best to help the child drill on her weak spots in the day's lesson. But if the parent recalls the principles of abstraction and trust, the parent might instead choose to review the child's triumphs, with some sympathetic words about the rough spots. Otherwise, the child will hear that the parent is disappointed and blame herself, even though the parent is trying to do the very best for the child. "Quality time" depends not so much then on whether the parent and child do something "special" and exciting together, but whether the little things that pass between them are validating at the highest level.

One of the most common guilt-ridden situations is when a parent has scheduled an event with the child and work priorities intervene. The child takes second place for a time, and we fear the negative messages. But we know that the child will be receptive to our genuine communication. We can explain our immediate priorities to him. We can postpone the immediate event, so long as we do not postpone the validating message. You can postpone anything but love.

Of course, if the event is one which cannot be postponed, such as the child's performance in a play, we must face the fact that if we miss it we have given a negative message. All the pleading in the world that it will never happen again, that we will take the child to some other extra event, that we will take off some extra time, will not substitute. Such pleading only strikes the child as false and invalidating. It may imply that we think so little of the child that we expect her to substitute an apple for an orange. Or it may imply that we are so riddled with guilt that we are out of control of our own lives. Whatever the implication most poignant to the child, it is far better to end the guilt and limit the damage by owning up to the conflict and asking the child to forgive us. It is only our perfectionism that holds us back here. As essentially spiritual beings, children forgive with tremendous grace when we just allow them to do so.

A final note on working outside the home. It can be a strongly validating experience for the child to visit our work place and even spend a day or a morning seeing what we do. Being included, knowing that we want him to relate to our work as he does to the rest of our life, can go far to help the child accept in a positive fashion the fact that we are not always available. And perish the thought that it is better to stay away or not to call when work obligations are pressing. Even a quick meal, a "hello-goodbye" visit, or a phone call can fill a negative void with a positive message. Out of sight, out of mind does not work at the most abstract levels.

Great as the pressures on the modern-day family are, a frequent return to the basic operating principles of the parent-child relationship will minimize their negative impact. Of course, there are limits to how little parental time a child can survive healthily without a parental substitute. Most important for a happy parent and professional combination is a clear sense of control over one's choices, the same sense we want most to pass on to our children.

With the kind of interaction that the operating principles suggest, we should be poised to detect early any strains on our children and to help them express them and interpret them or reassess our own priorities as need be.

You can postpone anything but love. Contrary to popular wisdom, the greatest career opportunity in the world will come around again, albeit in another form. Your four-, six-, or sixteen-year-old will not. Fear of lost opportunity at work is nothing compared to regrets about lost family life. And if you feel stifled and burdened by postponing ambitions while parenting, trying for superparent status may be much more taxing than looking at other options. A change of attitude might be all that's needed.

Perhaps you are unconsciously replaying old tapes from your mother, who felt trapped not because she would have done differently but because she felt she didn't have a choice. Or perhaps you have not placed enough trust in yourself and the unfolding of your life to accept that if loving your children is what you want to do right now, then it's OK and there will be time for the rest later. Or perhaps your desire for every advantage for your child—the best house, education, sitters, etc. that money can buy—prevents you from recognizing the most important advantage any child can have—loving parents who regularly show their love by giving their time and attention.

Each family must work out its own division of family functions—bread labor, leisure, and chores. Options are many. If we use the operating principles to clear our own minds so we can accept and negotiate with the personal needs and priorities of each family member, we can develop the division that is right for us and change it as our family and needs change.

CHAPTER 12

Shopping

GOING shopping is probably the most direct contact a child has with the world of money and business. Babies go to the store with their parents as soon as they go anywhere else out of the house. When we are in the market with our children, we have an important opportunity to help shape their perceptions of material goods, money, consumption, and advertising. Yet often shopping is a very trying time. The parent is likely to feel in a hurry because she would rather be doing something else. The child is responsive to the ubiquitous product promotions. And both parent and child tire easily and get on edge because of the sensory overload of colors, shapes, bright lights, strange faces, and innumerable little decisions about what to buy.

The simplest and yet perhaps the most useful step we can take is to begin to think out loud. We must not worry about what the neighboring shopper might think about us when we discuss the price of tunafish with a two-year-old. Never mind. The child will see us making careful choices and will come to appreciate the various factors which go into a buying decision. By doing our thinking out loud, we are setting an example for the child of how to consider buying decisions; we are helping him interpret the soft or hard sell marketing pressures that even the youngest child is receptive to; and we are speaking to him as if he matters at a time when he can easily feel wholly ignored. We should remember to speak to the child, though, not to ourselves. Look at the child's eyes and wait for a comment. The child will be delighted.

If we find that our child is continually bugging us to buy something specifically for him, we can easily get frustrated and angry. "But everything I'm buying is for you and the rest of us!" Instead of giving messages of frustration, we should try to assess whether we have allowed the child to participate enough in the shopping, so that he feels that it is for him. We can decide ahead of time what decisions don't really matter one way or another and let the child decide these. "Do we want vanilla or lemon yogurt?" "How many apples shall we buy?" "Should we go to the hardware store or the laundry first?" This kind of participation will mean a great deal to the child and can turn a negative experience into a positive one.

Often a child will see a particular product which really attracts her, especially if she has seen it on television or if a friend has one. We tend to panic when this first happens, thinking: "Oh, no! Here we go with the whining in the check-out line that all parents must endure." But we need not accept that any particular activity will always be a trial. Of course, there are bound to be negative experiences for us all. But every ordinary activity of our children has the potential to be a constructive experience if we make no negative assumptions and remind ourselves of the operating principles.

Often we must say no. But how we say it can be as important as the fact that we said it. If we feel frustrated, victimized by modern advertising or by our child, the child will feel either unloved or helpless. On the other hand, if we take the time to articulate why we must say no, we can speak firmly, with conviction, and give a rational reason if the child asks why not? We could say, "You have enough toys already," but usually this is not enough. It would be better to take the time to acknowledge her need to imitate friends or to please the cheerful advertiser on television.

Instead, we could say, "You would really like to have that truck, wouldn't you, because you thought it looked like a lot of fun on television. But they don't tell you on television how much it costs and that it will not really ride up the walls like that in most homes. Maybe we could spend more time playing with the trucks you have at home now."

Most children will be receptive to this kind of response. They may feel sad for a moment, but they will not feel deprived, unappreciated, or unloved. It is important to remember to carry through on our own constructive suggestions, though. In this example, we should be sure to remember to play with the child's trucks fairly soon.

If we plan to give reasons whenever our children ask why or why not, we may wonder if we are letting the children control us. After all, we should not have to account to our children for our actions, we might think. But this kind of fear arises from within us, not from any situation outside us. A child can never control its parents in reality. We can only *feel* controlled. We get this feeling when we let ourselves give knee-jerk reactions instead of thoughtful responses to our child. If we do this, she can manipulate the direction and focus of any interaction. She can touch on our sore spots, tug at any vague guilt we feel, spark our defenses, or embarrass us with our apparent inconsistencies. If we answer every question at the same level of abstraction as the child asked it or at a lower level, we are vulnerable to this kind of manipulation. We need also to avoid the Perry Mason syndrome: that the only real answer is a yes or no. Numerous examples in this book demonstrate that human communication is imperfect and if a direct answer to a question does not really address the concerns of the asker, it may be better not to give it.

The response used in the illustration above is on a higher level of abstraction than the child was using. It answers not only the question, but also some of the doubts which may arise as a result of our response to the question. We help our child interpret

our no by empathizing with her feelings and making it less likely
that she will interpret the denial as an expression of disesteem.

If we remind ourselves to trust ourselves as well as our children, neither will feel in a position of having to account to the
other or that either is trying to control the other. Instead, each
will be more inclined to listen to the other, and respond constructively. The tensions of a shopping trip are a special challenge
to thoughtful parenting. But a carefully handled outing into the
world can set a positive tone for the whole day.

It is worth making special mention of how the particular
level of spending which is common to a family can affect a child.
If we parents like to dress smartly, for example, we must be aware
that our child will feel most comfortable if we show our willingness to allow him to do the same. He may choose not to dress
like us for his own reasons, and that is fine, but he needs us to
give him the freedom to choose. Giving him discretion in matters
which do not threaten any real harm goes a long way toward
validating him. He is then more likely to be able to base his
shopping decisions on reasons which relate to his real needs and
wants rather than to vague insecurities about self-worth. In terms
of the operating principles, we are permitting the child to think
of shopping at its appropriate level of abstraction. The child will
be less likely to use buying to salve a wounded ego or to get
revenge and more likely to make rational decisions we can live
with and even be proud of.

CHAPTER 13

Watching Television

TELEVISION is like experience spoonfed in the guise of play. It is like experience because it shows pictures which resemble real life enough to make the child feel as if she is observing real life. It is spoonfed, because the child does not need to actively participate in any way to watch. And it seems like play because it appears to have minimal risks of harm and because it has artificial rules to limit it. The child sits in front of the television set out of harm's way, and the viewing activity is limited because we can turn off the set at any time and every show, no matter how serious the problems it portrays, ends in a half hour or so.

But this resemblance to play is merely a disguise because the child is not in control of the play. She has no choice in any particular situation how far to go or when to stop, as she does in play. Instead, the television thrusts upon the child experiences which are often far beyond her comprehension, with no interpretative guidance at all.

To illustrate, suppose the child watches a barroom brawl in a cowboy show. We suspect it is harmless. Good conquers bad every time and the injuries are usually minimally gruesome. But the child will learn other things. The saloon lady they are fighting over apparently needs men to stand up for her dignity. The hero as well as the bad guy quickly resort to violence to solve their differences. Neither the hero nor the heroine shows any sadness at the death of the bad guy, merely because they had "justification" for the violence. And no one spends any time eating, picking flowers, taking walks, talking to children, giving thanks for their blessings. Instead, the activities that determine whether someone is a hero or not are: seeking out problems that appear to be beyond peaceful resolution, interfering in other people's affairs, and being emotionally impervious to just about anything.

While this sounds like a particularly bleak portrait of a cowboy show, it does illustrate that television teaches at numerous levels of abstraction. There are a number of ways to see that television is more a positive than a negative experience.

First of all, at least a portion of the time when our child watches, we should watch with him to help him interpret what he sees. We can use commercial breaks as a time to start a conversation in order to bring out any questions he may have. We must choose our initial words carefully. If we say: "What do you think of this show?" we will get no response, or at best "Oh, it's OK." We need to break the ice by expressing our own feelings. We might say: "I felt happy when the guy in the white hat made the black-hat guy leave town." This kind of remark is more likely to elicit a real response. He might say: "Yeah. He saved the lady's farm, because the bad guy tried to burn it." When we share our feelings about the show, we have given the child a strong validation and have left him feeling important enough to share his feelings with us. If the child has a question, he is likely then to ask it. "But what happened to the horses that were trapped in the barn when it was burning?" That kind of concern, or something many times worse, can be the focus of wicked nightmares. If we have not been there to share our child's experiences, we are at a disadvantage when we try to help him come to terms with them.

A second way to see that television is a positive activity for our child is to help her choose which programs to watch. We should be careful to guide rather than command, to talk about choices rather than dictate them, to empathize rather than crit-icize. We can also set a positive example. If we want our children to be discriminating viewers and to turn off the set when there are no desirable shows, we must try to do likewise.

A third important step is to limit the total time for viewing. No matter how good the shows, the viewer is in a passive frame of mind. All experience comes to her without any participation on her part, when in reality the vast majority of worthwhile experiences come to us when we are in an active frame of mind and are actively participating with others in essential activities of life.

With television, our example is as important as at any other time. If we behave as couch potatoes ourselves and show no ambition to stay physically active and fit with exercise and outdoor activity, our child will be unlikely to do so either no matter how much we remonstrate. But if we are outdoors or engaged in physical activity, most children will tear themselves away from television, yes, even from video games, to join us.

Commercial messages on television deserve special consid-eration. As far as their impact on children, they may as well be treated like mini-shows in themselves. Each one pushes a prod-uct. But it also speaks on other levels. It pushes a particular life style. It pushes precise outlets for various abstract needs. It can place artificial spiritual importance on mundane, trivial things. We all can think of examples: The housewife whose day goes from gray to gay when a magic man from a can makes her floor sparkle; the bespectacled, meek young man who is suddenly able to relate to women because of his new car; the girl who feels insecure without her deodorant or maxi-pad; or the achiever who can't enjoy his triumphs without draft beer.

These sales pitches do not promise durable, functional goods to help us in our precise life activities, so much as they promise love, affection, confidence, friends, and success. We would prefer that our child look for these things within rather than without. Even with commercials, then, we should watch with our child whenever we can, help him interpret, and limit his exposure. If we are not with him when he watches, we should seek a caretaker or sitter who will not use television as her or his major assistant.

It is worth considering here the special impact which television can have on very young children, most notably through cartoons and the educational shows for small children. First of all, if we watch the cartoons that are available to children, we will find that violence is the norm and that heroes are alternately victimized and then all-powerful. It may not be desirable to have our toddlers spend so much of their time learning behavior patterns for situations which we hope will be few and far between. We must rid ourselves of the notion that family interactions are unexciting to the young child. If we give young children focused attention, they will choose our attention over some exciting children's show, almost every time. Likewise, a playful sitter can keep toddlers occupied and away from the television.

It takes a great deal of visual stimulation to keep the attention of a young child riveted to a television. This is why so many of television's educational shows for the very young have ever-changing bits of color and movement. They have numerous short skits and momentary visual pieces which change before the child has any real chance to understand or interpret them. The kind of concentration and persistence at a task which can give a real sense of satisfaction is virtually nonexistent. Similarly, the actors try hard to relate to the child by speaking and acting like many of the older kids and adults that he has observed. But many of the kinds of behavior they reenforce by making them seem cute and lovable can hurt others in real life, like gratuitous criticisms, putdowns, and ridicule.

These shows garner praise, because they actively seek to help interpret this kind of negative behavior. For example, they show how some grumpy, nasty monster is really just lonely and unsure of himself. But the shows seldom are realistic in showing how to accept the unpleasant character as he is. Usually the unpleasant character ends up admitting his feelings and setting everything right by a sudden if temporary change of heart. This rarely happens in real life. Rather than concern our child with how to make the monster see the light, we should have her learn how to deal with a monster.

To illustrate, an oppressive teacher or boss is not going to change overnight because we give him or her a surprise birthday party. We should be occupying our child with validating inter-actions which give her the self-esteem to keep her life under control even if her boss or teacher is a monster.

Kiddy shows and situation comedies alike focus repeatedly and approvingly on a behavior pattern which is particularly damaging according to the operating principles. That is, the putdown. How often the loudest part of the laugh track on any situation comedy is a conversation in which the speakers compete with sarcastic putdowns of one another. On kiddy shows, we often see the superior character shake his or her head contemptuously and secretly at some innocent error or clumsiness by a more sympathetic character. Even the cartoon characters are constantly playing dastardly tricks on each other and laughing when the other feels miserable. Do we really want our children to assume any of these roles?

It is worth noticing how much harder than normal it is to get a meaningful response from a child after a recent experience with one of these shows. Even a child who is used to thoughtful, validating interaction with parents can be temporarily turned to this mode of verbal noncommunication, turned to the "dark side," if you will.

To end on a positive note, few things are as wonderful for expanding a child's horizons and showing the richness and inter-dependence of life than some television shows. But we must seek out these special programs, and we still must remain ready to help interpret any observation with which he needs help. Once we decide to spend some time watching with our children, we may very well find that it is a great joy for us. Our confidence in our children will get a great boost when we hear the wonderful thoughts and ideas which our children develop on their own.

CHAPTER 14

Communicating

MOST of the examples in this book deal with the skill of communicating. This chapter will bring together the most important pointers on how to communicate with our children and how to guide them to communicate with us in a mutually validating way.

Children begin communicating immediately at birth, both verbally and nonverbally. Nonverbally, eye contact is one of the most powerful means of human communication, and a baby is capable of looking into our eyes and attracting our gaze right at birth.

Touching is another important way of communicating from the very start. The mother, father and baby are programmed to seek and enjoy each other's touch. Facial expressions are also very effective and meaningful for the newborn. Not only do babies imitate facial expressions in the first days of life, but they actually know whether different expressions are reassuring or threatening.

In addition to using their eyes, face, and touch, parent and child communicate with other body language. Each can tell easily whether the other is tense or happy, tired or excited. Whether a father clutches the baby gently or firmly, whether he acts as if he is coming or going, how closely he places his face next to the baby's, all tell the baby how he feels. Likewise, if the baby arches her back or stretches out her arms, he knows she is uncomfortable or in need of attention. These nonverbal communications do not lose their power when the child learns to understand and speak in words.

A baby communicates verbally too, though without words. Few can ignore the screeches of a determined baby. But parents are especially receptive to a baby's noises, even tiny whimpers. His cry of need is just about unbearable to them. In the case of a breastfeeding mother, the influence of hormones virtually compel her to come to him and make every effort to meet his needs. Conversely, his contented gurgles give special joy to his parents and reinforce their parental feelings of love. Many parents who are with their babies a lot in the first few months find that the communication is so effective that they rarely hear a full cry from their baby. Rather, they respond to various moans or whimpers before he needs to cry.

This kind of close communication need not be broken as the child learns to respond to precise words and then to speak them. If the parents talk openly to the child as if she could understand every word, the child will grasp the subtleties of tone, body language, and phrasing which mean so much even in adult communication, as well as the words themselves.

We have all heard adults who felt obliged to talk "baby talk" to babies. However, the more baby talk a baby hears, the more likely he is to use it when he begins talking. We also may wonder what the baby thinks when he observes that we talk one way to everyone else and another way to him. It is unlikely that this observation gives the baby a positive feeling about himself. We should therefore try to speak naturally to him and avoid "talking down" to him. Studies suggest that a higher than normal tone is pleasing to babies, but "baby talk" finds little justification.

It may also be worth noting that we should speak naturally not only in our vocabulary and pronunciation, but also in our grammar. Often when a baby first begins to make phonetic sounds, we feel tempted to teach her the names of everything in the room instead of just continuing to speak to the child in normal sentences. But this early emphasis on things and on the mere recognition and naming of things may place emphasis where we don't want it. True thought always involves sentences. Sentences focus on an *action* word which describes a *relationship* between two things.

If we view life as a process and creation as an interdependent whole, then we need to emphasize action and relationships rather than things and their names when we first guide our child into using our language. When we take this approach, it can be startling how truly abstract the thinking of a child can be. He seems predisposed to notice patterns and relationships of surprising subtlety long before he will concern himself with precise and independent things. If we think about survival and cultural success, the major goals of learning, the quick recognition of patterns of interaction between people, between things, and between people and things would be much more helpful than learning to recognize a whole list of things. It is no wonder then that a child is most receptive to communication in sentences.

To illustrate, when seven-month-old Natalie picks up a doll, we might say "Dolly! Dolly!" Instead, we could say, "Yes! You picked up your doll!" The first response might get the child saying "da-da" sooner, but the second gives her several relationships and patterns to consider. If she can pick up the doll, she can pick up other things. And if the doll is hers, that means a certain type of relationship, too. According to the operating principles, we can trust that when the child needs to say "da-da," she will. But meanwhile, we can see to it that she gets a positive and functional world-view.

Our children's sensitivity to nonverbal as well as verbal communication need not diminish with age. Perhaps it is because the child is still so receptive to all clues to meaning that children are so good at detecting falsehood, insincerity, and insecurity.

Rather than feel vulnerable before these seemingly intuitive powers of children, we can quickly learn to enjoy them and use them to strengthen our positive influence. We must be wary not to use them negatively, however. How many times have we seen a parent trying to control her child without words (so that no one will notice), by frowning across the table or across the room.

Chances are the child ignores the parent, sensing only a vague feeling of disapproval and insecurity, meanwhile wondering how odd it is that the parent is afraid to speak her mind in certain company.

The positive way to use nonverbal communication is to try to emit positive messages of validation in body language and with the eyes, even when we have to say negative things. Our body language can go far to reassure the child at the more abstract levels, even when we must communicate bad news to the child at some precise level. To test this idea, we need only consider how often people avoid looking others in the eye when they want them to feel especially bad. It gives the nonverbal message that they would rather not even "give them the time of day." When we avoid eye contact with our children, we will most likely communicate a message of low esteem, either for them or for ourselves. The child will be unlikely to pay much attention to our precise communication in the context of that kind of abstract message.

This book contains many examples of ways to use verbal communication in specific situations. Here we can identify all the communications tools generically that we might use when we want to ask our child to do or stop doing something.

First of all, we must look at the child. For the modern parent, this seems almost impossible sometimes. We are overloaded, as we juggle jobs, household management, family chores, bills, insurance reviews, conflicting calendars, and relatives' advice with our personal needs and desires to enjoy our spouses and children. To meet the eyes of our child just seems sometimes to take a minute we cannot spare.

But it is worthwhile. If it seems hard to believe that eye contact could be so important, we might make a trial. When we ask John to clean up his room, notice his response. "Ah, Daddy, not right now." If we say "Johnny," look at him, wait for him to look at us (the first couple of times it may be quite a wait), and *then* ask him to clean up his room, chances are he will say something like "OK. In a minute." The difference may appear subtle, but the feelings each has after the exchange are dramatically different.

If we seek eye contact, we will often find it necessary to use the child's name to get her attention. One's name is a very validating thing to hear. Also, if she knows that we will address her by name when we want her attention, she need not sustain an indefinite tension because at any minute her parent may make some demand or criticism of her. I use the label "everpresence" to name this vague feeling that a critical parent is watching or may catch us at just the wrong time or may make sudden demands. It is a serious deterrent to self-reliance, self-confidence, and intelligent risk-taking. It is best eliminated as soon as possible.

It is worthwhile to actively try to use the child's name more often. We should especially use it during the more relaxed, joyful conversations. Most of us can remember people in our pasts who used our name or a certain form of that name only when they were critical of us. The negative messages tend to linger on for many of us.

Once we address our child by name and look at him, already we are likely to have a better perspective on our own thoughts and feelings, as well as on his. The next step is to see that our bodies are speaking positively at the abstract level. Are my arms folded as a defense against my positive feelings in an effort to appear stern to him? Is my body half turned, so that I can pretend that he does not have my full attention? Am I fidgeting with something for the same reason? A closed posture will threaten him, so that he will muster his defenses and be preparing to parry my words rather than listening as I speak. In contrast, an open posture will tend to disarm him, so that he will not get his ego defenses up and can be more responsive to what I have to say.

When we begin to speak, we should try to reflect what we have seen or heard, rather than beginning with our criticism or request. We should acknowledge the current state of being of the child. Perhaps the child is angry. Or she is so happy that she is making a lot of noise. Or she is absorbed in reading. Or she has stopped eating. Whatever she is doing, if we acknowledge it, we have gone a long way toward having an enjoyable, constructive exchange. If we can, we might suggest a factual reason for the child's feeling or activity, as a further sign of our esteem for the child. "You're mad because Dick has your train." "You are all excited because your friend is coming over this afternoon." "You are absorbed in reading because you are pleased you can read so well." Or, "You have stopped eating because you are starting to feel full." After such a statement, we must wait patiently for a response. It will almost always come, even if it takes some time. The child must be allowed to accept our good feelings. Gratitude is a very important emotion which is much too often ignored. We need to let the child sense his appreciation of us. (We can stand some validating, too.)

After we have addressed the child by name, after we have focused our gaze on her, after we have empathized with the child's feelings, after we have waited patiently for a response, and after we have received one, then, and only then, is the ideal time to say what we originally had in mind. That same thought which we might have blurted out impatiently through the side of our heads to the back of the child's head with no constructive effect and with only a vague uneasiness to mark the exchange, is now likely to have the desired effect. Using the examples above, we can now say: "I would like you to work your problem out with Dick." "Please try to make less noise. It's getting on my nerves." "I would like you to stop reading now and come to dinner." Or, "It is important to your health that you eat more of your vege- tables."

If it seems as if this kind of conversation is just too time consuming, we need to remind ourselves to trust that doing our best as parents will not only help the child but will also benefit us. Even on the dimension of time, we know that a stitch in time saves nine. Loving communication even at the busiest mo- ments is likely to decrease the number of times that the child demands great blocks of time to overcome a tantrum of confusion, a bout of low self-esteem, a stand-off of resentment, or a period of total rebellion.

Of course, the need for eye contact and positive body lan- guage is just as strong when the child initiates the conversation as when the parent initiates it. We can hardly expect the child to look up receptively when we address her if we do not do the same. Even if we must say: "Just a minute," or "Not now, I'm busy," the child is far more likely to accept our communication on the level at which we intended it if we look up and smile.

It is worth mentioning that when we speak, we should speak out and not trail off or mumble. The latter behavior suggests that even we ourselves do not think what we have to say is very important, so why should the child listen? It also suggests to the child that we have a low opinion of ourselves. It is extremely hard for a child to maintain her self-respect if her parent is without it.

Closely related to the need to speak up and out is the need to stop speaking when we are finished. Children are likely to view repetition as an implied slur on their understanding, if not a deliberate provocation or sign of lack of self-control on our part. We should not repeat ourselves or ramble on. Rather than list innumerable reasons for our position, it is better to take a moment to think and then give the most important or persuasive of our reasons.

Finally, again closely related to these difficult skills of speaking up and stopping when we are finished, is the effective use of silence. Several times in this discussion, the parent has been left waiting. Waiting for a response is not a bad thing. Sometimes we think we should expect instantaneous responses from our children as a sign of respect and attention. But could that kind of expectation be why so many of us feel compelled to say "Uh" before each sentence? Is it that we fear a valued listener (a parent) will give up on us before we have composed our response? We can trust our child to think a moment in order to give us a valuable response. Our silence while we wait communicates that trust. Even silence can be a strong validating communication.

Another important communication tool we parents have is the use of words that name or describe our child. We should avoid using negative labels for our child, because the child is unlikely to be mature enough to hear that it is merely an expression of our anger and not a reflection on him. We should try to avoid words like "lazy," "brat," "pain in the neck," "idiot," "stupid," "clumsy," "selfish," "crazy," "smart-alec," and "handful of trouble." If we must use descriptive expletives, let them be more or less neutral, like "amazing," "funny," "strange," "silly," "something else," "a thousand surprises," and "energetic."

Of course, we should try to use positive labels whenever we can, such as "great," "cutie," "lovebug," "smart," "ingenious," "helpful," "delightful," "fun to be with," "cooperative," "nice," "kind," "strong," "loving," "pretty," "neat," and many more. We also can help expand the child's sense of her own potential by using a variety of other labels when they are appropriate. But none should be repeated too often, lest the child see them as stereotypes, predictions, or limitations rather than as potentials. These might include: "artist," "bike-rider," "writer," "cook," "well-mannered," "thinker," "busy," "relaxed," "runner," "talker," "reader," "good at math," "scientist," "mechanic," and so on. We must be cautious to avoid ever generalizing in a bad way about these names. It may be validating to tell a five-year-old working with a hammer that he is a good carpenter. But we must avoid saying something like, "Well I can see you will never be a carpenter." This is a powerful door-slammer in a child's mind.

Still another powerful skill of parental communication is to repeat what our child says. Even when we think we need a very sophisticated response, just repeating what he has said back to him can often carry the conversation just as well. The repetition signifies that we listened, we understood, and we value the statement. For example, if Jim says, "I don't like you anymore," we may be hard put to respond. But if we merely say, "You feel like you don't like me anymore," it is surprising how easily the child will go on with the conversation from there and usually in a more constructive direction.

In the case of a child just learning to talk or read out loud, repetition is the most effective way to reinforce the successes while subtly correcting any errors. Suppose Ginger says, "I didn't see the cat when it comed in." There is a big difference between saying, "You mean 'came,' " and saying, "Oh, you didn't see the cat when it came in."

A final note we can make about communication skills is that we should always keep in mind the great power of a yes as opposed to a no. It is not too simplistic to remind ourselves that yes is the essence of an affirmative communication, while no is the essence of negative communication. We should try to increase our yeses and decrease our nos, no matter what our child says. Suppose, for example, that Gerry says, "Mom, I want to take my umbrella. I think it is going to rain." It is a bit cloudy, but I know that it will be a sunny day, and to carry Gerry's umbrella all over the shopping mall would be a tremendous burden. I could easily say, "No, you can't. It is not going to rain." That is all true, but I have given three negatives. I could say, instead, "Yes, it almost looks like it might rain with those clouds in the sky. But the weatherman said that the sun would come out. We are going to be in the mall most of the time. I think that we will not need the umbrella." All of that is true too. But I have used only one negative. I have been affirmative with respect to the child's efforts to anticipate her needs and to interpret her environment.

If this chapter has sounded more like a discussion of parents' communication rather than children's communication, it is no mistake. We cannot make our children communicate a certain way. They are programmed to communicate, and our job as parents is to allow their skills to develop with as helpful guidance as we can give.

Communication is the primary tool of the parent and the primary learning activity of the child. Exploring and experiencing its potential powers are among the great joys for both.

CHAPTER 15

Healing

WE seldom think of healing as a major activity of childhood. But when we think about it, we are often amazed by the healing capacity of a child's body. It is also common knowledge that children are amazingly resilient emotionally. This is an important healing function, too. So, even though the child does not often consciously decide to engage in a healing activity at any given time, it is worth considering how we can participate with our child in healing whenever it occurs.

A common question among parents is how much sympathy we should give to a child who has been injured. If our toddler Miranda falls and scrapes her knee, we have a number of options. We can pick her up and cuddle her, kiss the injury "to make it better," and hold her until she feels good again. We could make an objective assessment of the injury, and, seeing that it is not serious, minimize the event, saying, "It's not bad. It will go away fast. Come on, let's go." We might criticize the child for being inattentive, in hopes of discouraging future falls. Or we could make an assessment of the whole event, including the physical injury and the resulting pain, and help the child accept and interpret both. We might do this by stooping down to the child rather than scooping her up and by saying, "Oh, you fell! That must hurt a lot! Let's see how bad it is. That kind of scrape goes away fast but it really hurts a lot just when it happens." We can consider these four options in turn.

The first option seems to exaggerate the event. Some say that exaggerated sympathy may encourage future clumsy acts as a way of getting validation. Of course, if the child is well-validated otherwise, she will merely wonder why you exaggerated the event. But if sympathy is a major emotion between the parent and child, we perhaps should be concerned. The solution, however, is not to withhold any sympathy, but rather to see that we use other events and emotions also to communicate our love to the child. We might be wary of kissing the injury to make it better, lest the child get an exaggerated picture of our powers. Again, the answer is not to withhold the kiss, but rather to let the child know that we are helping heal the emotional injury, the pain, not the physical injury. We could say, for example, "I'm sorry you got hurt. Maybe a kiss will help you feel better faster."

We probably would choose the second option in response to Miranda's fall with the thought that we want the child to be tough, so that she will not cry if she sees that she is only slightly injured. Unfortunately, this strategy may well backfire. According to the operating principles, the child feels fully her essential emotions. If we deny them or ignore them, the child will indeed get the message that she should be tough. But she will also get the message that she is not tough, that her emotions are bad, and that she should try to hide them or suppress them. If other emotional outlets are not regularly available, a child whose emotional wounds are treated this way may well explode with vague unidentifiable pain at unforeseen times.

We would choose the third option again for purposes of teaching the child a certain lesson beyond the event itself. We would criticize clumsiness so that she will try harder to avoid it. But if we apply the operating principles, we can see that the child will hear first the message that we think she is clumsy. We are allowing no room for human error. She is unable to live up to our expectations. Consequently, she feels spiritual pain in addition to the emotional pain prompted by the fall. We can use the principle of trust to reassure ourselves that the injury and pain are enough to discourage future falls, to the extent that she can prevent them.

The last option, then, seems the most appropriate. It validates the child's feelings and acknowledges the injury, but does not exaggerate the event. If we try this kind of approach to an injury, we will find that it is also the most comfortable and enjoyable for the parent. We are meeting the child's needs as simply and genuinely as we can.

We are also setting an important example for effective healing behavior. It is well known that the most effective healers, whether doctors, nonprofessionals, or spiritual leaders, owe their success to sympathy and gentle guidance, combined with accurate information and a clear expression of trust that the injured person will heal and quickly become whole. Early in their lives our children have the opportunity to act in a healing way toward others, whether it be playmates, pets, garden creatures, or parents. All their lives, a good sense of the healing power of validating messages will not only help them help those around them, but it will help them heal themselves.

Another common aspect of healing is our child's visits with doctors. Just as with the scraped knee, it is important that we guide the child in his interpretation of what is going on. We should remember that doctors are not God. They do not have the healing power. Rather, they know a good deal more than most of us about how to assist the healing powers within us. If we happen to have a doctor who behaves in a way contrary to this interpretation, it may well be worthwhile to consider changing doctors, even if we are satisfied with the doctor's handling of the physical aspects of childhood. It is important that the child retain his sense of control over his own body, as an essential part of his being.

We should seek expert help whenever the problems of our child have gone beyond our capacities as parents. We must select a doctor we are comfortable with as a family and then work with him or her to facilitate healing. Tending to our parenting skills will increase the effectiveness of any therapeutic treatment. We are uniquely situated to help our child accept her condition, accept the assistance of the doctor, tolerate any pain in the treatment, understand the course of recovery, and express any feelings she has, whether positive or negative. Even in cases of major surgery or prolonged hospitalization, attentiveness to the operating principles can help make the difference between an emotionally defeated, vulnerable patient with continuing physical and mental complications and a validated one who "springs back almost as if nothing had happened."

It is most important that we not underestimate the depth of the young patient's fears, the possibility of feelings of rejection, guilt, or abandonment, and the capacity for curiosity, questions, and comprehension concerning what is being done to him and why. Once his parents open up to him in appreciation of these things, they may well find that he has enough courage for his own needs and even a bit left over to share with them.

In our own relationship with his doctor, we should seek to understand and feel confident about any treatment not only for our own sakes but also so that we can pass on these feelings to our child, who is the person most directly involved in his healing. Parental support in healing by staying close and involved does not mean that we should take over the nurse's or doctor's duties. It is better that we remain the comforter and reassurer and not take on the responsibility, for example, of giving shots or changing bandages out of an excessive zeal to control the whole process. We must consider that if there is pain in recovery, the patient, particularly a young one, may get mixed messages if the parent tries to take on both medical and comforting duties. It is probably best to let it be clear to the child that there has been no change in the parent-child relationship, and that when the doctors or nurses are gone, so will be the medical procedures.

Even with prolonged illness or physical disability, healing with the help of the operating principles helps the child and the family accept the condition and prevent it from spreading negativity to any parts of his life beyond those necessarily involved. Since none of us is perfect, a child who has an imperfection which is a bit more obvious or disabling than the average child still has every reason to develop as a well-validated, self-assured person.

The spirituality of the child gives the child another amazing healing tool—the capacity to forgive. By being forgiving ourselves, and by allowing the child to forgive herself for errors which caused injury, we are allowing the child to develop this God-given capacity. The chief way we can help the child to forgive herself is to make sure that when the child makes an error, we address any criticism at the precise level of the error and be sure that the child remains properly validated at the more abstract levels. The child is then free to accept her error, rather than deny it as a matter of self-defense. Once she accepts the error, she can go about learning how to correct it or avoid it next time. A willingness to forgive also will give our child the enviable power to bring better health to those around her, ultimately creating greater joy for herself.

Another healing power that children use unknowingly is prayer, in the sense of recognition that there are forces beyond our individual control which affect our lives, in the sense of gratitude for life and all the good we enjoy, and in the sense of willingness to attend to those aspects of our lives over which we do have spiritual control. A young child who feels validated is one continuous prayer in that he is not easily side-tracked from the spiritual essentials of his daily life. We marvel that a child can go from tears to laughter in the blink of an eye. But this is a manifestation of this ability to transcend the precise moment in favor of abstract spiritual reality.

The child's power to heal, to forgive, to accept the best in any of us, gives parents a special gift of grace. No matter how much negative feedback we have been giving him, no matter how awry our well-intentioned lessons have gone, no situation is beyond hope or help. The lower his self-esteem, the more patience we will need and the more suspicion we will have to overcome when we start to speak positively to him. But if we allow him to heal and to become whole by acknowledging his wholeness and spirituality, he will heal.

For healing to be most effective, we should think through

our own assumptions about how body, mind, and spirit relate to one another. For the child, they seem like one indivisible unit. With the new discovery of meditation and exercise as essential complements to a well-trained mind, it seems that our cultural values may also be putting greater emphasis on this unity. The best way to encourage our children to address their needs in all three dimensions at once is by example. If we have favorite ways of exercising our bodies, we should share our activity, goals, and triumphs with our children. If we meditate, worship, or recall our spiritual selves some other way, such as by uplifting reading, by ceremony, by music, or by conscious relaxation, we should share these activities, too. If our work and reading keeps our minds growing, we should share our satisfaction with our children.

Our children may not ultimately choose the same activities we have to maintain their internal unity. Our job, though, is to acknowledge the need and expose them to the various options, so that they can choose which precise behaviors are best for them.

The mutual healing powers of child and parent could stand a lot more attention than we generally give them. Mutual healing is one of the unique joys which parent and child can share.

CHAPTER 16

Understanding Death

BECAUSE of children's tendency to respond to the essentials in life, they are aware of death very early in life. They see bugs stop moving when we swat them. They see people killed or cartoon characters pretending to be dead on television. They see old people and wonder if they are going to die. They know they were born and sense that there is an end when there is a beginning. They ask how many birthdays they will have. And they see flowers and leaves die every year. They soon figure out that the chicken we had for dinner was once alive. They detect the terror in our voices when they climb a ladder. There is no denying them that death is a part of life.

It is most often from us that our children first learn that they ought to feel uneasiness, fear, or dread of death. Most children do not fear the dark until we let them know that we expect it of them. What seems fear of the dark before these messages is usually reluctance to have us leave them at night. They begin to identify the feeling with darkness only when someone tells them about ghosts, goblins, monsters, or burglars. It is the same with death. Children have a sharp eye for patterns and for principles. They expect a beginning to lead to an end, a circle to come all the way around, a human creature to have the same life passages as any other creature. Their curiosity about death is not necessarily related to the uneasiness most adults feel.

There is no reason, then, to try to shield children from the fact of death when they begin to ask questions about it. When they ask about their own death or that of loved ones, we may wish to reassure them that life is long and full before death, but the mere fact that we are here enjoying our lives and are a good five times older than they are is reassuring in itself.

Death by violent means, by accident, or by disease is harder to explain than death of old age. Death by violence includes crime, starvation, persecution, and war. When we are trying to maintain a loving attitude toward all people, we must also acknowledge that there are destructive people and that even normally constructive people can destroy each other. The best we can do is to come to terms with these questions ourselves and share our concerns bit by bit in answer to our child's questions, or when the child needs help interpreting his observations. It is most important to be genuine, not overly dramatic, and willing to admit when we are ignorant or confused ourselves.

Fear of death can be paralyzing. Many experts believe that the potential for nuclear war may be paralyzing many of our young people. But fearless acceptance of natural death as a part of life, coupled with an abiding faith in the human potential that can surmount man-made and unnatural threats, may well allow our children to bring an end to the reign of nuclear terror. As parents we can promote both this acceptance and this faith in our children. By shaping our actions according to the operating principles which this book describes, we can foster the kind of inner security which will free our children from the endless quest for absolute security on the outside. Our children may be able to develop a world environment which is based on trust and mutual validation of peoples.

As for death by accident, we parents play an important role in protecting our children from accidental death and should not deny that sudden death is a risk and does happen. Children are relatively quick to understand the importance of avoiding visible risks of death, such as a cliff, a lake, or a sharp object. It is our job to keep a watchful eye to see that they do not get momentarily distracted when they are near even an obvious risk. We must also protect them from invisible risks, such as poison, speeding cars, abused chemicals, or radiation, until they are old enough to comprehend the nature of each risk.

When we give warnings about accidental death, we may mistakenly try to emphasize the risk by making death seem more terrible. Gruesome descriptions of what might happen are more likely to create fear and nightmares than to enable the child to avoid a risk. Rather, we should explain precisely how the risk might turn to reality and how it can be avoided, so that the child will have the necessary information to help him avoid the risk.

Death by disease cannot be hidden from our children either. If a friend or relative is ill, the child's perception of essentials will prevent him from being deluded that the sick person is well. As with his own bouts with illness, he will be least damaged by an undramatic but genuine explanation of the state of health in language he can understand. Likewise, we must exercise discretion in sharing our private worries or grief, but we do him no favors if we deny or try to hide them when he senses their presence.

Once we accept that there is no hiding death and that our willingness to listen and share is most important, we can make thoughtful decisions about how much death and mayhem we will expose our child to on TV, in movies, or in print. If we are in touch with our own sensibilities, we will model for our child the value of protecting personal serenity and peace of mind no matter what tragedy may exist elsewhere. We may find that even the front page of the city newspaper is unacceptable to be left around the living room. This does not mean the child will be thoughtless or ignorant of the trials of others. Constant exposure to violence with no power to overcome it breeds fear and inertia, not righteous action. Also the fear of death does not protect us nearly so well as our love of life.

Most cultures have developed ceremonies to deal with the fears and sorrows associated with loss and death of loved ones. We should allow our children to share in these to the extent that they can comprehend them with the help of our interpretation.

We should use our discretion to subdivide these ceremonies into the parts which are appropriate for our children and the parts which are not.

If we are attentive, we will discover that mourning is a natural process to a child for dealing with death and loss, even though our society is only recently coming to grips with it. The stages of denial, anger, bargaining, acceptance, and renewal often come more naturally to a child than to us. If a pet dies, a favorite toy is lost, or a friend moves away, we need to trust the natural mourning process and not try to orchestrate or suppress it. At such times the child needs our presence if wanted, our listening, our acceptance, and our empathy. We should not confuse sympathy with empathy. If we try to feel their anger or hurt, we may be caught up short when the child responds, "You don't know! It wasn't your dog!" Instead we need to sense what the child is feeling and affirm it as a valid feeling. We cannot force acceptance and renewal but we can make them come more easily by validating feelings.

The hope which stays with children so perseveringly because of their spirituality can be a great joy to us parents at times of death. Dying is one of the activities about which we may learn as much from our children as they learn from us.

CHAPTER 17

Making Music

Making music is an important activity for children. Children often begin singing before they can talk. The musical tones of their voices seem to be as intriguing to them as the phonetic sounds they can make. Even if their parents seldom sing to them, they will usually make up their own songs. Songs often accompany play.

Likewise, children dance as soon as they can walk and will rock on their knees even before that. They enjoy rhythms from birth and pound them out as soon as they can hold something in their hands. There is evidence that babies respond to rhythm even before they are born. The sound and feel of the heartbeat of the mother, so close to the fetus for nine months, is apparently one of the more soothing aspects of the mother even after birth. It seems likely that the rhythm of the heartbeat is the prototype for all musical rhythm. When a father carries a baby, holds him so that he can feel him breathing, or rocks him, he exposes him to other natural rhythms. All of these have a magical power to calm and relax the baby.

Though this deep influence of music continues throughout our lives, we seem to understand very little about how and why music can move us so. Long after Christmas is over, for example, children will delight in even one hummed line of a Christmas carol. Many of us can recall whole symphonies of feelings and memories when we hear a few bars of some song which we knew well in our childhood. The harmony, melody, and rhythm of music seem to have a special relationship to the workings of our minds.

Being so close to their basic spiritual essence, children tend to take full advantage of the spiritual power of music. Parents need to allow time and opportunity in our children's lives for them to use music however they see fit. We can place our trust in their intuitive sense of how music will help them grow as spiritual beings, and we must allow them a free choice of what kind of music they prefer.

Of course if the noise level becomes a burden on others or repetition is driving us crazy, we should let the child know it. But we should be careful to distinguish between objection to her choice of music and objection to her choice of a way of expressing it. Children will generally accept the fact that we must all respect the needs of each other and that we can pursue our desires only so long as they do not persistently limit someone else's freedom to do the same.

But we need to avoid throwing in an objection to the type of music: "Why do you listen to that terrible music anyway?" She is likely to respond only to the attack on her taste and aesthetic freedom and ignore our otherwise reasonable request that she reduce the noise or repetition.

In addition to allowing our child to pursue his musical inclinations, we can share our own with him. Even if we don't like each other's music, we can share our common delight in music itself. Though the child may tease about our old-fashioned tastes, we need not justify or defend them. It is enough if we acknowledge our differences and refer to the more abstract level on which we can agree that music is important to us both. This way we parents can make sure that music is a source of validation rather than a source of tension in the household. It is too important an instrument of emotional and spiritual communication to waste by imposing negative connotations on it.

Just as we avoid dictating the type of music our child enoys, we should try not to dictate the type of instrument which she prefers. We must follow the cues of the child about when she would be interested in learning an instrument and which instrument it will be. If the child begins to bang on pots and pans, this does not mean that the child will be a drummer. Nor does it mean we must put a set of drums on her Christmas list. It may mean only that the child feels like exploring what she can do with rhythms. Or it might mean only that the child has used her mind to discover something to do with pots and pans, since cooking is still not available to her. Likewise, we cannot assume that our child will benefit by piano lessons at three because we always enjoyed the piano.

As with other activities of the child, our role as parents is to expose the child to the various options in musical expression, to communicate to him by our example the value we place on the music, and to do our best to validate the child in general and in connection with his precise choices about music. We should avoid second-guessing whether he is a musical genius or whether he should be playing the violin or the cello. If we take care to expose him to these and to listen to him, he will let us know what is best at any given time in his musical life.

Because music is such a universal and relatively nonthreatening activity, it is a good one to practice our conscious parenting on. Singing a song with the children, dancing around the room for a moment hand in hand, or twanging rubber bands together, all can produce very good feelings between parent and child. Music and the movement it stimulates can also turn a tense situation around, by calling both parents and child back to a more abstract level of consciousness, back to basic human rhythms and soothing tones. Spontaneous dance is unlike almost any other physical activity in the way it tends to relax the body and get the mind, body, and spirit moving together. It seems a shame that our culture so seldom affords the opportunity for families to dance.

In our own homes, we can all play music and dance as much as we want. We should keep in mind that music can transcend all words and can speak directly to our essential being. We can call on music to bring us together with our children.

CHAPTER 18

Moving

THE experience of moving to a new house can be traumatic for a child, but it need not be. If she has come to rely on specific cues in her home or immediate physical environment or neighborhood for her self-validation system, a move may be extremely unsettling. On the other hand, if the focus of her validation system is on movable aspects of the family—possessions, pets, parents, and siblings—moving will be more like another example of life's continuous process of change, which a well-validated child accepts easily.

We can do a lot to help the child see a move this way. We can include her in the planning, telling her our thinking and creating manageable choices for her to make. Would she like to pack her books or toys first? Where should we set up the swing set? Does she think we should take the sandbox or buy a new one?

The little extra time we spend creating these ways for the child to participate can save both time and pain when the time for moving comes. She feels not only our general esteem for her, but also our esteem for her in connection with the precise activity of moving. The child will have no vague feeling that the move has something to do with her, or with the activities, accomplishments,

167

wrongs, or fears of her life. Rather, she feels secure that the essential elements of her world will remain intact.

We often worry that a change in schools may stop the child's progress or destroy his social confidence. At these times, we need to call on our principle of trust: If the child generally feels good about himself, he can handle the experience with a minimum of disorientation. Sometimes we are so concerned with the possible impact of a move, that we may switch our priorities unconsciously and cause the very insecurities that we are seeking to avoid.

For example, if the mother and father choose to live apart until the end of the school year for the sake of the child, seven-year-old Alex may be happy to finish out the year with his friends. But the familial relationships and the child's relationship with his father generally are more significant to a child's self-esteem than his relationships at school. Alex is likely to feel that a move which changes family life so drastically is a mixed blessing at best. At worst he may blame himself or his schooling for the break-up of his family and for the fateful move. Even if we explain to the child that we view his schooling as that important, guilt may well still abide. Alex may feel in the dark about why his schooling is more important than his parents' relationship. Is the tail wagging the dog? It may make him wonder how school, where he goes to be with his peers, have fun, play games, and learn skills, has the power to break up his home, even temporarily. And as for the relationship between his mother and father, which he has always sensed to be permanent, is it so easily given up?

Before we set the stage for these kinds of complications, we need to be very sure that we have not unknowingly shifted our priorities or accepted someone else's priorities as our own. We should listen to our in-laws, our children's teachers, and anyone else who wants to help, but then we must let our hearts guide us.

It is worth considering too that although a child wants and needs lots of attention, it is a heavy burden to carry to be the pivotal point for all family life. It is indeed important that we consider our child's future in all our decisions. But we should question whether any decision which brings real spiritual pain today can really promise any advantage tomorrow.

Children seem to know that childhood is a preparation for things to come. Otherwise, their free spirits probably could not endure the long period of dependence and training that family life provides. But if it appears to the children that we parents are totally absorbed in their future, this suggests that their future too will center around their children's future. They may well wonder if anyone ever lives now, today. The ability to make the best of today and to enjoy every minute is a God-given gift to children. We should think twice before we teach them, by our example, to give it up.

Many of us parents today carry with us twinges of guilt about the "sacrifices" our parents told us they were making for us. We may also have a nagging difficulty interpreting these memories. Do they mean that responsible parenting requires that we feel we are making sacrifices? Or is there another way to look at it? Perhaps we can spare our children this guilt that we feel, by really finding out whether something we think we should do as a sacrifice for the good of the child is really what we think it is. We might do well to trade in the word "should" for the words "want to" or "choose to." Though this is a subtle difference in attitude, it can make the difference between a parent who feels martyred and self-righteous and a parent who is happy and at ease with his or her chosen role.

A new home, like other major adjustments in family life, can challenge our assumptions about the way we make decisions and what we really want out of life. The operating principles can help us keep our perspective on the role our children play in those decisions.

Once we have sorted out the broader implications of the move, there is still a lot we can do when the busy day arrives to smooth the transition for everyone. As with every other activity, we can separate moving into its component parts, refining it until we reach a level where there are discrete activities that our children can share in. Carrying a few things into the moving truck, helping to decide which way to lay the rug, and helping to unpack can be very reassuring to the children. These special activities can also produce precious moments for the parents in the course of an otherwise grueling day.

CHAPTER 19

Traveling

TRAVELING is a very common activity for children and their families. The children are inclined to treat it as an adventure as long as we see to it that it does not threaten their positive world-view. But often we goal-oriented adults fail to recognize the actual process of traveling from place to place. We tend to think only of our destination. We forget that a day seems a good bit longer to a child than to us, and that a day in an airplane or in a car without a good idea of where we are going could be a hair-raising experience even for us.

It is important then to include our children, no matter how young, in the planning and scheduling of a trip. We can tell them where we are going, what we will do, and whom we will see. This will help validate them generally: We think they are important enough to know about and help plan the trip. We can let them help pack. We can let them make any decisions for which either alternative will do. Should we take four or five pairs of socks? Should we take the red or the blue belt? Which books should we take? Which side should we pack the hairbrush on?

Telling them about the trip and involving them in the preparations is not enough, however. We must be aware that the child sees the abstract level first. The precise preparations and anticipation may be very exciting, but the child may have little understanding of what is really going on. Does he really remember from last year what a vacation is, for example? His concerns may well be different this year from last year, even if he remembers a prior trip. More abstract questions may plague him if we do not think to answer them ahead of time.

For example, will things be the same when we get back? Are we coming back? How long is three weeks? Is everyone else going away too? We need to start at the beginning, at the most abstract level when we introduce any unusual event into our family life. We might explain why we take vacations, for example. It may not be self-evident why we need to get away if life is already good. We can also be sure to tell them how long we will be gone and that we are coming back at the end of the trip. Otherwise, uncertainties about the impact of the traveling may interfere with the child's enjoyment and our own.

Indeed, if we find that a child is getting very irritable, seems troubled, or acts uncooperative on a trip, we should not assume that she is not enjoying the trip or let vague guilt about our decisions respecting the trip take control of us. Rather, we should check whether the child has let the trip slip out of proper perspective, out of its proper level of abstraction. If we run through the above aspects of the trip to help refer her back to an understanding of the big picture, the child will more than likely "snap out of it." It is hard to go down to the beach every day and sit in the hot sun, when you are three years old and don't know if you will ever see your cat again.

Two other aspects of travel can be dealt with here: Should we take the children with us, and how do we stop the bickering en route? The operating principles help us to set our priorities on the first question. Because it is natural and safe for children to be with their parents, we must trust that our children would like to be with us, no matter how trying the experience would be and no matter even what they might say, unless they have experienced major separation before. Knowing this, we can dispense with make-weight considerations about what the child would most enjoy and address our own real needs and wants.

Is it time that we parents had some time together alone? Might we miss our children too much to feel comfortable, no matter how much we would like to enjoy the time alone? Would the children understand our needs and enjoy their alternative activities enough not to take the separation as a personal rejection?

As our alternatives come into focus, we can make a much sounder decision than if we spend our deliberations second guessing our children's needs. Perhaps we can spend part of our vacation time with the children and try a weekend on our own. Creative solutions come when we recognize that we have choices and that "the good of the children" rarely if ever determines an issue.

As to the bickering en route, we must consider this a special instance of communication problems, no matter what the favorite subjects for bickering are. Whether siblings fight, parents and children get on each other's nerves, or parents get at odds over how stern to be with the children or some other subject, we should always try referring the participants to a higher level of abstraction. Most likely, someone is feeling invalidated.

The commonest reason for lack of validation in a car is easily ignored, because we spend so much of our time today sitting side by side instead of facing each other that we take it for granted. But a principle source of tension in a car, airplane, or even a movie theater is the lack of eye contact. How long can you keep a positive attitude in a conversation when the other person will not look at you? Even traveling home from school can be a tense time for this reason. When the child has not seen his mother or father for some time, he needs most some of the nonverbal validation: touching and eye contact. If the father or mother does not make an effort to give these, the child may get more and more sullen as they proceed home and end up unable to communicate once they arrive.

Similarly on a long trip, pulling over to the side of the road and just looking the child in the eye for a few happy moments while talking about just about anything can do wonders for making the trip tolerable and even enjoyable for everyone. Even if these stops make the trip longer, they will have a positive effect overall. It is not the absolute length of the trip but the attitude of the people on it that has the most influence on whether it is a joy or a pain.

Traveling can be a positive experience for both parent and child if we take the time to let it be so.

CHAPTER 20

Laughing

L AUGHING is a frequent activity of children. Usually it is a great joy to us parents to see our children laughing, and we have few problems with it. However, sometimes we feel that we are being laughed at or that we do not know how to share our children's laughter. Also, sometimes we think that our children should not be amused when they are. Can the operating principles help with these delicate matters?

The principle of abstraction is a key to understanding laughter. Most things that strike us or our children as funny are essentially sudden shifts from one level of abstraction to another when the observer does not expect it. Laughter overtakes us when we recognize the shift. That magic moment of recognition breaks the tension of our bodies and minds which concentration on one level of abstraction has generated. We break into laughter. The biggest laughs come from the greatest shifts. If the lead sentence or question forces us to focus carefully on a specific level, a dramatic shift gives us a great release. If we are asked, "Why did God rest on the seventh day?" we conjure up our religious training, our cosmic sense, and anything else we can bring to bear on the question. When we admit we don't know, we hear the answer. "Because he was too tired to create the eighth." No matter what the joke, there is always a split second of puzzlement. Then we see it. The joker has put God down on our level. He has imagined that God could get tired, like any mortal. It is not this idea which is particularly amusing but the shift itself. We feel a total release of tension. This punchline in fact has another joke in it which could make us laugh again as we are laughing. In addition to suggesting the absurd idea that God could be tired, the punchline also jumps back up to the pure abstraction that in fact God could have created an eighth day then and there, before the seventh, if He had chosen to. From the cosmic to the mundane and back makes for a good laugh.

Children tend to have magnificent senses of humor. This is because they move so easily between levels of abstraction. They are learning on every level and are willing to talk and think on any level at almost any time. This accounts for the fact that sometimes they find jokes we think hilarious to be not particularly funny at all. Usually this happens because they have not experienced that moment of tension. The shift in levels of abstraction was obvious to them.

When we feel our children are laughing at us, we can get furious very quickly. It usually happens when we are angry already. What is probably happening is that the child has shifted levels on us. They see that we are angry but that the anger is only about some foolish little thing. Or they have noticed something on a precise level which stands in stark contrast to our strong emotions, and it affords them a little release of tension. We all have experienced the snicker when a pompous speaker trips over a wire on the podium. The child takes advantage of these moments, too.

These need not be taken personally. In fact, we can use them ourselves to reference ourselves to a more appropriate level of abstraction. If we find ourselves getting intolerably angry, we can seize on any small thing to change tension to laughter. "Did you see the cat jump when I just yelled?" Everyone can relax and come to terms with the real problem and not the harsh messages of anger.

When we feel that we are missing out on our children's

merriment, again we need only try to make our own sudden shifts in levels of abstraction. A child who is not used to his parents participating in her laughter may think it odd at first. But if we do not let pride get in our way and we persist in our efforts, she will soon accept us and share her laughter with us.

As for what we consider inappropriate laughter, such as ridicule of ethnic or disadvantaged groups, the macabre, or the dirty, the best approach is to minimize our reaction and trust that the child will not ultimately enjoy this kind of humor as much as healthier kinds. We should make our feelings known, but we should not add interest or tension to the situation by indicating that this kind of laughter will provoke an instant dramatic reaction from us. Rather, we can explain quietly why humor at the expense of others may seem funny, but that the humor is outweighed by the hurt and imposition on those at whose expense we might laugh. We can assume that the child will be receptive and we can wait until the fashion of the moment leaves on its own. Like any other disfavored behavior, we do not want it to assume implications of greater import than the precise behavior itself, or it may hang around a good bit longer than it would have otherwise.

We should do our best to laugh with our children and to help them laugh. One sure way to do the latter is to be silly occasionally ourselves. Even our children can be caught unaware when a serious, busy, more or less self-controlled parent stands up and strikes a goofy pose. There are few things more strongly validating and exhilarating than the resulting universal laughter.

CHAPTER 21

Living and Loving

L IVING and loving have been the primary focus of this book. Both parents and children are in a continual state of unfolding, of becoming increasingly ready for life to reveal itself in its true essence. We all hope that our children will do more than merely exist, merely pass their time on this earth. We would like them to think, feel, believe, help, share, and love, as we ourselves want to do. We hope to spare them from the tougher lessons of our lives and save them time by passing on the benefit of our experience. At the same time, we want them to be whole beings, able to meet life's challenges with faith, ingenuity, integrity, energy, and a clear mind.

It is not our responsibility to create all this in our child. Luckily for us, the major work of creation has been done. Our job is to make the best of ourselves as parents. We must concentrate on taking joy in being parents and on allowing our instinctual love for our children to blossom into a strong validation system. It is very easy to do both, but almost impossible to do either one alone.

Life with a child can be a continuous celebration of life. As adults we tend to compartmentalize our lives, saving celebration for special occasions. We often associate celebration too with physical excesses that would be a disaster if we tried to use them any more often than we do. For children it is the daily background of good feeling and love that is most nurturing, not whether her birthday party was a success or her Christmas exciting enough. For this reason this book has focused on everyday activities that often get less of our attention than the traditional celebrations.

But formal celebrations too can be a powerful validation in a child's life. We need to plan our traditional religious and ethnic holidays openly and together around the needs and desires of the family and each individual in it. We need to let our family traditions evolve, trusting our own unique program. We can add our own special days or moments, including birthdays, anniversaries, favorite family events, pets' birthdays, weekly family nights, and so forth.

We need to choose ways to celebrate that strengthen our spiritual connections to each other and that nurture our health and our sense of family community. We need to avoid unnecessary excesses and the exhaustion of making a "big production" every time or at times we will resent it. Then the experience of frequent celebration will remind us how much we have to celebrate and help us join in the natural celebration of life that is a child.

The first two operating principles remind us that loving is the central focus of a child's life. If possible, it will be the child's main activity, coexisting with every other activity. The child's very sense of identity is dependent on loving. Because the child is a spiritual being, he or she can ultimately only affirm his or her existence by experiencing the essential spiritual function of loving. For the self-validating child-person, "I love, therefore I am."

It is our job as parents to keep a home in which life and love will thrive through careful nurturing, acceptance, and validation. We might take a cue from the three famous oriental monkeys, who see no evil, hear no evil, speak no evil, and do our best to "see only love, hear only love, speak only love." If this sounds ostrich-like, we must consider it in the context of the operating principles. Whenever we try to apply them, we find that we are aiming to maximize the good side of our children, ourselves, or any situation, while carefully keeping the negative side in its proper perspective. Following our example, our children will benefit by a positive view of the world. With a positive view of themselves and the life around them, the children can bring joy to themselves, to those around them, and to us.

Only a positive view of life will motivate our children to reach out for life's experiences and to those in need of love, rather than waiting for some outside force to bring experiences to them or to make others love them. Without a positive world-view, the complexities and challenges, the future shock, and the sensory overload of our transition to the twenty-first century will surely keep them down.

With a positive world-view, our children can welcome new opportunities, experiences, people, and places. They will have a strong validation system, operating first from parents and then from within. They accept the interdependence of all creation and look forward to their creative part in it. They take joy in the littlest as well as the greatest of life's manifestations. They feel hope more often than fear and love more often than contempt. They accept the diversity of life and take joy in its revelations. They accept change as an essential part of life, without feeling any threat to their identity. And they enjoy the age they are today, remember with happiness the past, and look forward with joy to the future.

These goals sound ambitious. We may fear that we will be merely substituting new kinds of guilt for the old tried and true ones. But we need to remember that good parenting is a process, not a goal. As long as we are trying, we will not fail. Our children, as essentially spiritual beings, will respond to our efforts and graciously forgive our imperfections.

When I told my four-year-old daughter that my book was called "You can postpone anything but love," she screwed up her face in bewilderment.

"What does that mean?" she asked.

"It means you can put off anything until another time except seeing the good in life and in the people around you."

"What does that mean?" she asked again.

"It means you don't have to do everything now, but you do have to love the people you are with."

"So we should love each other!" she said triumphantly.

"That's right," I said proudly.

"So we just became friends!" she said gleefully.

Suggested Reading

Pregnancy and Childbirth
Brewer, Gail. What Every Pregnant Woman Should Know.
Brewer, Gail. The Pregnancy After 30 Workbook.
Dick-Read, Grantly. Childbirth Without Fear.
Hazell, Lester. Commonsense Childbirth.
Korte, Diana and Roberta Scaer. A Good Birth, A Safe Birth.
Leboyer, Frederick. Birth Without Violence.
Sousa, Marion. Childbirth at Home.

Breastfeeding
International Childbirth Education Association. Nursing Mother's
    Manual.
Jelliffe and Jelliffe. Human Milk in the Modern World.
Kippley, Sheila. Breastfeeding and Natural Child Spacing.
La Leche League International. The Womanly Art of Breastfeeding.
Pryor, Karen. Nursing Your Baby.

Baby and Child Care
Brazelton, Berry. Infants and Mothers: Differences in Development.
Gesell, Arnold and Frances Ilg. Infant and Child in the Culture of
    Today.

Hymes, James. The Child Under Six.
Newton, Niles. The Family Book of Child Care.
Spock, Benjamin. Baby and Child Care.
Spock, Benjamin. The Problems of Parents.

Parenting

Bettelheim, Bruno. Dialogues with Mothers.
Briggs, Dorothy. Your Child's Self-Esteem.
Campbell, Ross. How to Really Love Your Child.
Craig, Sidney. Raising Your Child, Not by Force, but by Love.
Crary, Elizabeth. Without Spanking or Spoiling.
Daley, Eliot. Father Feelings.
Dodson, Fitzhugh. How to Parent.
Dyer, Wayne. What Do You Really Want for Your Children.
Faber, Adele and Elaine Mazlish. How to Talk So Kids Will Listen
    and Listen So Kids Will Talk.
Faber, Adele and Elaine Mazlish. Siblings Without Rivalry.
Ginott, Haim. Between Parent and Child.
Greenspan, Stanley. First Feelings.
Kaplan, Louise. Oneness and Separateness.
Pruett, Kyle. The Nurturing Father.
Rogers, Fred. Mister Rogers Talks with Parents.
Sears, William. Creative Parenting.
Sears, William. Growing Together.
White, Burton. The First Three Years of Life.

Education

Bloom, Alan. The Closing of the American Mind.
Dennison, George. The Lives of Children.
Holt, John. How Children Fail.
Holt, John. How Children Learn.
Kozol, Jonathan. Illiterate America.
Kozol, Jonathan. The Night Is Dark and I Am Far from Home.
Miller, Alice. Thou Shalt Not Be Aware.
Neill, A. S. Summerhill—A Radical Approach to Child Rearing.
Shilcock, Susan and Peter Bergson. Open Connections: The Other
    Basics.
Sisson, Edith. Nature with Children of All Ages.

Family Life and Choices

Bellah, Robert and Madsen, Sullivan, Swidler and Tipton. Habits of
    the Heart.

Cahill, Mary Ann. The Heart Has Its Own Reasons.
Elkind, David. The Hurried Child.
Fraiberg, Selma. Every Child's Birthright.
Fromm, Erich. The Art of Loving.
Fromm, Erich. The Sane Society.
Holt, John. Teach Your Own.
Judson, Stephanie. A Manual on Nonviolence and Children.
Lappe, Frances. What to Do After You Turn Off the TV.
Lowman, Kaye. Of Cradles and Careers.
Macy, Joanna. Despair and Personal Power in the Nuclear Age.
Moynihan, Patrick. Family and Nation.
Subby, Robert. Lost in the Shuffle.
Thevenin, Tine. The Family Bed.
Trelease, Jim. The Read-Aloud Handbook.

Nutrition and Health
Cheraskin and Ringsdorf. Psycho-dietetics.
Coffin, Lewis. The Grandmother Conspiracy Exposed.
Crook, William. Can Your Child Read? Is He Hyperactive?
Feingold, Benjamin. Why Your Child Is Hyperactive.
Giller, Robert. Medical Makeover.
Hall, Ross. Food for Nought.
Hays, Louise. You Can Heal Your Life.
Randolph, Theron. An Alternative Approach to Allergies.
Smith, Lendon. Feed Your Kids Right.
United States Surgeon General. Healthy People.

Learning and Mind
Bateson, Gregory. Mind and Nature.
Bateson, Gregory. Steps to an Ecology of Mind.
Chomsky, Noam. Reflections on Language.
Gould, Stephen Jay. The Mismeasurement of Man.
James, Muriel and Dorothy Jongeward. Born to Win.
Leakey, Richard. Origins.
Piaget, Jean. Structuralism.
Piaget, Jean. The Language and Thought of a Child.
Reiser, Morton. Mind, Brain, Body.
Rico, Gabriele. Writing the Natural Way.
Winson, Jonathan. Brain and Psyche.
Wolf, Fred Alan. Star Wave: Mind, Consciousness, and Quantum
    Physics.

Spirituality and Inspiration
Capra, Fritz. The Tao of Physics.
de Chardin, Teilhard. The Phenomenon of Man.
de Lubicz, Schwaller. Nature Word.
Fox, George. Faith and Practice.
Fulghum, Robert. All I Really Need to Know I Learned in
     Kindergarten.
Gawain, Shakti. Creative Visualization.
Jampolsky, Gerald. Good-Bye to Guilt.
Kushner, Harold. When All You've Ever Wanted Isn't Enough.
Nearing, Scott and Helen Nearing. Living the Good Life.
Peale, Norman Vincent. The Power of Positive Thinking.
Peale, Norman Vincent. You Can If You Think You Can.
Peck, Scott. The Road Less Traveled.
Powers, Thomas. The Great Experiment.
Powers, Thomas. Invitation to a Great Experiment.
Schuller, Robert. Tough Times Never Last, but Tough People Do.
Siegel, Bernie. Love, Medicine, and Miracles.
Watts, Alan. The Way of Zen.

Psychology
Freud, Sigmund. Psychoanalysis.
Jung, Carl. Man and His Symbols.
Masson, Jeffrey. The Assault on Truth: Freud's Suppression of the
     Seduction Theory.
Piaget, Jean. Structuralism.

Self-Help
Fromm, Erich. The Art of Loving.
Harris, Thomas. I'm O.K., You're O.K.
James, Muriel and Dorothy Jongeward. Born to Win.

Cultural Anthropology
Kitzinger, Sheila. Women As Mothers.
Leakey, Richard. Origins.
Mead, Margaret. Cooperation and Competition Among Primitive
     Peoples.
Montagu, Ashley. Growing Young.
Montagu, Ashley. On Being Human.
Montagu, Ashley. Touching: The Human Significance of Skin.

Cooperation and Peaceful Conflict Resolution
Cornelius, Ruth. All Together: A Manual of Cooperative Games.
Frank, Jerome. Sanity and Survival.
Heisberger, Jean. Christian Parenting.
Heisberger, Jean. Peacemaking: Family Activities for Peace and
    Justice Handbook.
Lifton, Robert. The Broken Connection.
Shilcock, Susan and Peter Bergson. Spaces for Children.

Special Issues for the Family
Elkind, David. The Hurried Child.
Kempe, Henry and Ray Helfer. The Battered Child.
Mack, John. Vivienne: A Study of Adolescent Suicide.
Parents Anonymous. I Am a Parents Anonymous Parent.

Children's Book Catalogues:
Chinaberry Book Service. 3160 Ivy Street, San Diego, CA 92104.
Enlightened Environments. P.O. Box 1408, Durango, CO 81301-
    1408.
Hearth Song. 2211 Blucher Valley Road, Sebastopol, CA 95472.

Index

A

Abandonment, 157
"Absolutely not", 41
Abstraction, levels of, 22–26,
    38–39, 46–47, 93, 101,
    115–116, 142, 166, 174–
    175
Acceptance, 13, 17, 150
Accidents, 161–162
Achievement, achievers,
    107
Addiction, 61
Advertisements, 77, 136–138,
    142
Affection, 100–101
Affirmation, 17
Aggression, 77
Alcohol abuse, 37, 61, 122
Alienation, 59
Allergies, 77
Allowance, 30–33, 34, 70, 98

"Already has a mind of her
    own", 40
"Amazing", 152
Anal character, 94
Anger, angry, 24, 32, 59, 126–
    127, 137, 149, 175
"Angle", 23
Anniversary, 178
Apologize, apology, 23, 26
Approval, 16, 116
Arbitrary rules, 43
Artificial, 44
Assertiveness, 17
Attention, 16, 109, 116–117,
    143, 149
Attitude, 4, 11, 24, 42

B

Baby, 3–4, 34, 58, 72–74, 78,
    83, 101, 125–126, 136,
    146–147, 164

Baby talk, 146–147
Ball, 42–43
Barroom brawl, 140–141
Bathing, 83–87
Bathroom, 91–96, 101
Beat, conflict over, 126
Bed, bedtime, 35, 69–75, 112
Bed-wetting, 77
"Because I said so", 56, 79
Beginning schooling, 117–118
"Better get used to it now", 14
Birth, 3–4, 34, 40, 145
Birthdays, 80, 143–144, 160
Blame, 128
Body language, 18, 24, 46,
    145–146, 148, 149
Bonding, 35
Bored, 35
Bouncing on beds, 112
Boundaries, setting, 39, 41–42,
    43–44
"Brat", 151
Bread, arranging of, 29
Breastfeeding, 35, 146
Bribes, 15
Business, 136
"Busy", 20, 28–29
Butterflies, children as, 33
Buying, 136–139

C

Career, 134
"Care-free youth", 19
Car, cars, 41, 58, 162, 170–
    173
Carrots, preparing, 35, 105
Cartoons, 143–144
Cat, 171, 175
Celebration, 177
Ceremony, 159, 161

Character, "It builds
    character", 56
Check, checking, 44
Chemicals, 162
Child abuse, 97, 101
Childbirth, 4
Choice, 31, 44, 167
Clean, cleaning, cleanliness,
    47–48, 83–87
Clean up, 41, 49, 87
"Clean up your room", 48,
    148
Clothes, 88–90
"Clumsy", 151
Coat, outside without a, 62–63
Cold, 34
Commercials, 77, 141, 142
Communication, 4, 14–15,
    19, 35, 38–39, 52–57,
    69, 145–153
Competitive, 117
Compliments, 32
Components, 104–105, 169
Compromise, 9, 25, 44, 85–
    86, 126–127
Concentration, lack of, 77
Confidence, 32, 41–42
Conflict, 46–47, 112, 126–127
Control, 24, 29, 33, 35, 40–
    45, 111, 115–116, 130,
    134, 138, 156–157
Cookies, 25
Cooking, 104
Cooperative, cooperation, 23,
    28, 36, 86, 105, 126–129
Correcting errors, 24–25, 151–
    152, 158
Courage, 121, 157
Courtesy, 104
Cowboy show, 140–141
Crafts, 112

Cravings, 77
"Crazy", 151
Creation, 177–180
Crime, 37, 161
Criticising, criticism, 23–24, 51
Crying, 77
Crying, baby's, 34, 73
Cuddle, 154
Cue, 32, 35, 78, 166
Culture, cultural patterns, 3–6, 35–37, 58–59, 78–79, 92–93, 117, 147, 159
Curiosity, 157
"Cutie", 152

D

"Da-da", 147
Dance, 164, 166
Danger, dangers, 40–44
Dating, 44
Death, 37, 50, 141, 160–163
Deception, 19
Decisions, decisive, 31–33
Defensive, defenses, 25, 138
Denying, denial, 19, 31–32
Dessert, 79–81
Diet, dietary, 76–82
"Didn't you hear me?", 23
Dinner guests, 27–28
Dinner chairs, rattling of, 27
Dirty, 47, 95
Disability, 157–158
Disagreements, 36, 126–127
Disease, 157, 161
Distrust, 19, 47, 113
"Do as I say, not as I do", 59
"Do it right", 106–107
Doctors, 156–157

"Doesn't miss a thing!", 18
"Dolly! Dolly!", 147
"Don't bother me now", 20
"Don't play with yourself", 98–99
Double standard, 59–60, 62–63, 79
Drawing lines or limits, 43–45, 86–87
Dreams, 108–109
Dress, dressing, 32–33, 47–48, 88–90
Drinking, 60–61, 122–123
Driving, 104, 170–173
Drug abuse, 37, 122

E

Eating, 31, 76–82, 149
Educational shows, 143
Embarrassment, 10, 57, 128
Empathy, 32
"Energetic", 152
Environment, 32, 43, 83–84, 99, 108, 114, 169
Errors, correcting, 24–25, 151–152, 155–158
Essentials, essence, 3–7, 15, 17, 20, 166, 178
Exaggeration, 116, 155
Example, teach by, 62–63, 86, 100, 112, 122, 128–129, 131–132
Exercise, 159
Expectation, 32, 38, 51, 52, 70, 85, 94
Experience, 19, 22, 111, 142
Experimentation with sex, drugs, alcohol or cigarettes, 122

Explain, explanations, 23, 56–
57, 99
Explain-and-divert, 56–57
Eye contact, 101, 145, 148–
149, 150, 172

F

Facial expression, 58, 145
Failure, fear of, 107
Fail, failure, 31–32, 38–39,
106–107, 120–121
Faith, 13, 24, 65, 111
Fall causing injury, 154–156
Famine, 37
"Fantastic", 116
Favors, doing of, 26
Fear, fears, 15, 19, 25, 28, 37,
43–44, 74–75, 91, 95,
101, 121, 139, 157, 160,
161
Fear of the dark, 160
Fear of failure, 107
Flexibility in play, 111–112
Focused attention, 16, 28, 143
Food, 76–82
Force, 30, 31–32, 70, 74, 91,
92–94, 97
Forced learning, 32
Forgive, forgiveness, 11, 26,
60, 92, 134, 158
Freud, 9, 92, 94, 98, 103
Friends, 36, 44, 129
Frowning across the room,
147–148
Frustration, feelings of, 32, 57,
59, 73, 137
"Fun", 152
Fun, 25, 32
"Funny", 152

G

Game, games, 15, 109–110,
111
Garbage, 106
Genuine genuineness, 25,
116–117
"Getting her way", 25, 86
Genitals, 98–99, 101
"Giving in", 14
Good, goodness, 5–7
Gratitude, 105–106, 150, 158
"Great", 152
Guidance, 14, 27–28, 32–33,
40–45, 98–99, 101
Guilt, guilty, 24–25, 28, 71,
92, 109, 128, 133–134,
168–169, 171

H

Habit, habits, 62, 75, 90, 92
Hate, 24
Healing, 154–159
"He did it!", 127
"Hello-goodbye", 134
Helping, 104–107
Helping of vegetables, 24
Holidays, 80
Homework, 115, 131
Housework, 3
Hope, 11, 158, 163
Horses in the barn, 141
Hug, hugging, 29, 100–101
Humphrey Bogart film, 110
Hunger, hungry, 34–35, 76–
82
Hurry, 106
Hyperactivity, 77

I

"I didn't do it!" 127
"I knew you couldn't do it", 50
"I love you", 101
"I thought so", 50
"Idiot", 151
"It was nothing", 105
"It wasn't me!", 128
Illusions, 15
Imitation, 57, 58–65, 94
Impatient, impatience, 24, 32, 43, 57, 150
Indulgence, 26
Infections, 76–77
Injury, 154–156
Instinct, 4
Instruction, 113
Intelligence, 18
Internalize, 15, 39, 45, 107
Interpreting, 18–20, 28, 108
Irritable, irritability, 77, 82, 171

J

Jokes, 175
Judge, judgmental, 7, 16, 120–121, 126–128
Judgment, trusting one's, 31
"Just a minute", 150
"Just for me", 48

K

"Kind", 152
Kiss, kissing, 16, 100, 154–155
Knee injury, 154–156

L

Labels, positive and negative, for the child, 151–152
Ladder climbing, 160
Laugh, laughter, 4, 20, 22, 29, 112, 144, 174–176
"Lazy", 151
Learn, learning, 3, 5, 23–24, 30, 31–32, 52–54, 108–113, 114–123
Learning disabilities, 77
Levels of abstraction, 21–26, 27–29
License, 14–15
Limits, limiting, 15, 43–45, 112, 152
Listening, 17, 32, 98, 123
Lonely, 34
Love, 6, 8–11, 12–13, 22, 28, 100–101, 116–117, 120–121, 177–180
"Lovebug", 152
"Luck", 31

M

"Make it better" after injury, 154
"Make it up to you", 23, 25–26
"Making peace", 109
Making a pie, 105
Making music, 164–166
Manipulated, 128, 138
Media, 58
Meditation, 159
Mess, 41, 49, 56
Messages, 15, 22–25, 46, 55, 61, 80–81, 93, 98–99, 125, 155

Mind, 159
Mischievous, 16
Mistake, mistakes, 38–39, 59–
   60, 107
Money, 136
Moodiness, 77
Motivation, 30
Mourning, 162
Movies, 102
Moving, 167–169
Multiplication tables, 115
Music, 119, 151–153, 164–
   166

N

Name, using the child's, 148–
   149
Neatness, 87
Negative, negativity, 14, 23,
   28, 111, 151, 157, 165
Negative world-view, 13, 28
Negative messages, 24–25, 42,
   46–49, 93–94, 98–99
"Nice", 152
Nightmares, 37, 77, 162
"No", 14, 41–42, 56, 137–
   138, 153
Noise, 146, 150, 166
Nonjudgmental, 16, 32
"Not now", 150
"Not old enough", 60
Nursing, 35, 146
Nurturing, 49
Nutrition, 76–82

O

Observation, 18–20, 108, 110
Oedipal complex, 103
Oral character, 94

P

Packing, 167, 170
Pain, emotional, 5, 27–28,
   156–157
Painting, 117
Participation, 104–107, 136–
   137
Party, 28, 123
Passages, 4
Pasteur, 84
Patience, 11, 14, 23, 43
Peers, peer pressure, 77, 122
Penis envy, 103
Peace, 109, 112
Perception, 18, 21–22, 23–24
Perfect, perfectionism, 59, 116
Performance, 16
Perry Mason syndrome, 138
Persuasive, persuasion, 24
Pets, 156, 167
Phone call, 134
Piano, learning to play the, 31,
   166
Picking up toys, 87
Play in the street, 41
Play, missing of the, 133
Play, playing, 42, 108–113,140
Pleading, parental, 48–49, 92
Please, desire to, 46–51, 52
"Please", 31
Poison, 162
Positive messages, 23
Postpone, 99, 133
Potential, child's, 33
Pots and pans, rhythm on, 166
Praise, 12, 16, 38, 105, 108,
   116–117, 143
Prayer, 158
Precise, levels of precision, 21–
   26, 111, 115

"Pretty", 152
Private, privacy, 95, 98, 99–100
Professions, 4, 152
Prohibiting, 44
Promises, 28
Promotions, 136
Protection, 161–162
Prove themselves, 120
Punishment, 52–54, 126–128
Putdown, 144
"Putting on a show", 16

Q

Quarreling, 109–110
Question, questions, 19–20, 97, 103, 112, 141

R

Rain, playing in, 24–25
Reading, 31, 35, 149
Reading as validation, 29
Rebellion, 82, 150
Receptivity, receptive, 52–57, 79, 100, 133, 147
Referencing, 27–29, 82, 85, 98, 175
Reinforcement, 7, 16, 28, 71, 143
Rejection, 28, 47, 157
Relate, relating, 57, 143
Relaxation, 159
Religious tradition, 5
Reminding, 85
Repeat, repetition, 151, 152, 165
Revenge, 53
Reward, 80

Rhythm, 3, 164, 165, 166
Ridicule, 176
"Ridiculous!", 89
Risks, 40–44, 161–162
Rolling over, 74
Romance, 11, 44
Routine, 70–71
Rules, 5, 128

S

"Sacrifices", 169
Sad, sadness, 25
Salad-making, 29
Scapegoats, 60
School, 36, 115, 117–122, 168
Scolding, 9, 57
Seat-belting, 20
Security, inner and outer, 161
Self-assured, 158
Self-assertiveness, 64
Self-centeredness, 8
Self-confidence, 32
Self-conscious, 24, 47
Self-esteem, 10, 15, 25, 31, 39, 42, 49, 65, 92, 95, 103, 144, 150, 158
Self-fulfilling, 47
Self-image, 47–48
Self-motivated, 36
Self-validation, 13, 73, 167–168
Self-worth, 24, 116, 130
"Selfish", 151
Separation in hospital, 34–35
Sex, 10, 97–103, 122
Sexual perversion, 37, 101
Sharing, 6, 32, 106, 127, 128
"She started it!", 128
Shoes, leaving around, 22
Shopping, 136–139

"Should", 128
"Shouldn't", 120–121
Show, showing off, 16, 116
Siblings, 36, 57, 112, 125–129, 172
Silence, 151
"Silly", 152
Silly, silliness, 29, 112, 176
Singing, 164, 165, 166
Sitter, 142, 143
Situation comedies, 57, 144
Skills, 112, 152
Sleep, sleeping, 3, 36, 69–75, 109
Smile, 4, 151
"Smart", 152
Smoking, 62, 122
Snicker, 175
Socializing, 124–130
Songs, 102
Spank, 57
Species, characteristics of human, 5, 19, 25, 92, 114
Spending, 139
Spiritual, spirituality, 3–7, 19, 70, 101, 117, 130, 158–159, 165
Stages of development, 32–33
Stamps, licking, 106
Standing ground, 25–26
Stereotypes, 103, 110, 152
Stimulating environment, stimulation, 32–33, 110, 143
"Strange", 152
Strangers, 129–130
Street, playing in, 42
"Strong", 152
"Stupid", 23, 151
Stuttering, 77

Sugar, 76–82
Suppress emotions, 155
Surgery, 157
Survival, 8, 35, 116, 147
Swearing, 61
Sweets, 76–82
Sympathy, 25, 154–156

T

"Talking down", 146
Tantrum, 150
Teach, teaching, teacher, 63, 113, 114–123, 142
Television, 77, 102, 110, 137–138, 140–144, 160
Tenderness, 117
Tests, 119–122
"Thank you", 31
Thanking, 105
Thinking out loud, 136–137
Time, timing, 28, 30–33, 34, 44, 57, 86, 105, 130, 150–151
Toilet training, 9, 31, 35, 91–96
"Tomorrow", 25, 28
Tone of voice, 46, 51
Touching, 3, 22, 100–101, 145, 172
"Trap", 23
Traveling, 170–173
"Trick", 23
Trips, 170–173
Truck, buying toy, 138
Trust, 11, 31, 34–39, 75, 77, 84, 85, 86, 92, 95, 98, 107, 115, 120, 135
Trustworthy, feeling, 31, 34–35
Truth, 7, 19

Turning pages, 106
Two-career families, 132–135
Typing, 104

U

Umbrella in Paris, 26
Umbrella on shopping trip, 153
Unconditional, 16–17, 116,
    121
Unity of mind, body, and
    spirit, 4, 7, 159
Unreal, 13, see also illusion
Using the toilet, 91–96

V

Vacation, 170–173
Validation, 7, 12–17, 22–23,
    49, 51, 105, 121, 141,
    148
Vegetables, helping of, 24,
    105–106
Vices, 59
Victimized, parents by
    children, 29, 118, 137
Violent, violence, 37, 126,
    140–141, 143, 161
Violin, 166

W

War, 37, 161
Warning, 19, 100, 115, 162
Washed face, 24
Washing, 83–87
Watching television, 140–144
Weight, low or high for age,
    77
"What's wrong with you?", 23,
    38
Whisper, 28
"Why?", 37, 99, 137–138
"Why not?", 137–138
"Women are all alike", 110
Wonder, 20
Words, 146–147
Working, 106, 131–135
Working outside the home,
    106, 132–135
World-view, 9, 12–15, 19, 40,
    55, 170
Worship, 159

Y

Yelling, 23, 28, 57
"Yes", 14, 26, 41, 42, 106,
    138, 152–153